TRANSLATION:
AN INTERPRETIVE
APPROACH

This volume is a translation of Part I of Jean Delisle's *L'analyse du discours comme méthode de traduction : Initiation à la traduction française de textes pragmatiques anglais, théorie et pratique*, published by the University of Ottawa Press in 1980.

Translation Studies/Cahiers de traductologie is a collection of works on translation, interpretation, terminology, and writing techniques under the general editorship of Jean Delisle, Brian Harris, and Roda P. Roberts.

The collection includes the following titles:

No. 1. Delisle, Jean and Lorraine Albert. *Guide bibliographique du traducteur, rédacteur et terminologue/Bibliographic Guide for Translators, Writers and Terminologists*, 1979. 207 pp.

No. 2. Delisle, Jean. *L'analyse du discours comme méthode de traduction : Initiation à la traduction française de textes pragmatiques anglais, théorie et pratique*, 1980. 282 pp.

No. 3. Roberts, Roda P. (ed.) *L'interprétation auprès des tribunaux : Actes du mini-colloque tenu les 10 et 11 avril 1980 à l'Université d'Ottawa*, 1981. 201 pp.

No. 4. Delisle, Jean. (ed.) *L'enseignement de l'interprétation et de la traduction : de la théorie à la pédagogie*, 1981. 294 pp.

No. 5. Thomas, Arlette and Jacques Flamand. *La traduction : l'universitaire et le praticien*, 1984. 427 pp.

No. 6. Collectif de l'École de traducteurs et d'interprètes. *Bibliographie de Traducteur/Translator's Bibliography*, 1987. 332 pp.

No. 7. Mezei, Kathy. *Bibliography of Criticism on English and French Literary Translations in Canada/Bibliographie de la critique des traductions littéraires anglaises et françaises au Canada*, 1988. 177 pp.

Translation
s**T**udies
T
––
8

JEAN DELISLE

*L'analyse
du discours
comme méthode*

TRANSLATION:
AN INTERPRETIVE APPROACH

TRANSLATED BY PATRICIA LOGAN AND MONICA CREERY

FOREWORD BY DANICA SELESKOVITCH

University of Ottawa Press

Ottawa, Canada / London, England

Canadian Cataloguing in Publication Data

Delisle, Jean
Translation: an interpretive approach

(Cahiers de traductologie = Translation studies; 8)
Translation of Part I of: L'analyse du discours comme méthode de traduction.
Bibliography: p.
ISBN 0-7766-0155-5

1. Translating and interpreting. 2. Discourse analysis. I. Title.
II. Series: Cahiers de traductologie; 8.

P306.5.D4413 1988   418'.02   C88-090391-0

UNIVERSITÉ   UNIVERSITY
D'OTTAWA   OF OTTAWA

Translators' Acknowledgement

We would like to thank Ingrid Meyer and Brian Mossop for their expert advice
and Jean Delisle for his invaluable assistance.

The University of Ottawa Press gratefully acknowledges the assistance of the
Canada Council's Translation Grants Program in the translation of the
English edition of this work.

Contents

Foreword

The information explosion that is the hallmark of our age has resulted in a ferment of translation activity. Technical, scientific, administrative, and legal texts that in earlier times were never reproduced in another language are today being translated, while proportionally fewer works of literature are being translated. In order to keep up with this ever-expanding mass of multilingual information, researchers are trying to develop machines that can translate. Because the methods of text analysis that served literary translators so well cannot be applied mechanically, it has become necessary to translate language itself. As a result, a number of linguistic theories of translation have been put forward. Attempting to do more than explain machine translation, these theories have proposed models for human translation that completely ignore the extra-linguistic knowledge the translator automatically draws on in exercising his craft.

Theorists and practitioners have thus gradually separated into two camps, but the veiled hostility of the latter toward the former has not always had the result of producing theoretically convincing explanations of translation. Jean Delisle's work does. This professor of translation, who teaches at the University of Ottawa, has made a significant contribution to the theory of human translation. In his thesis, defended at the Université de Paris III in December 1978 and published here in book form, Delisle shows that, although knowledge of languages and their workings is essential to the translator if he is to understand the original text and render it intelligibly, it is not in itself sufficient to explain the translation process. That process involves innumerable cognitive complements that together with the linguistic significations create in the translator's mind the meaning he then attempts to re-express in another language.

The object of translation is meaning, taken in its full sense, which is much broader than semanticists and linguists have so far acknowledged. As the translators and interpreters associated with the École Supérieure d'Interprètes et de Traducteurs de la Sorbonne Nouvelle, Université de Paris III, push their studies further, it becomes increasingly apparent that meaning is in fact the object of language and the focus of communication.

Jean Delisle is to be commended for having clearly defined his field of study. For legitimate methodological reasons, he sets aside literary translation, in which re-creating the text is as much a matter of sensitivity to language as of rendering concepts in another tongue, and "pedagogical translation," by which a foreign language is analyzed so that all its aspects and workings become apparent. The purpose of pedagogical translation is to teach a language, not to communicate messages contained in texts. Its goals are not the same as those of translation pedagogy.

Professor Delisle has chosen to examine texts in which the conceptual content, rather than the artistic form, prevails—texts whose primary purpose is not to appeal to the emotions but to convey information. He has done so because they account for the vast majority of texts translated today.

Delisle calls these texts "pragmatic," and shows that the meaning they carry is not embodied a priori in the linguistic signs—though these will, through their syntax, make a semantic contribution—but is constructed by the speaker/writer and hearer/reader "from linguistic significations combined with non-linguistic factors." He then rigorously demonstrates that implicit in the idea that translations can be proposed on the basis of a comparison between languages outside of any communication situation is the assumption that a priori equivalents exist when, in fact, equivalence is established through comparisons drawn *after* the process of translation itself has been carried out. Thus, neither contrastive linguistics nor comparative stylistics can properly be said to be a method of translation. As Delisle rightly says, "The linguistic analysis carried out after the fact in comparative stylistics bears no relation to the cognitive process of translation."

We can only hope that it will soon be considered a truism to say, as Delisle does with some courage, that "in order to compare, one must have a point of comparison. In comparative stylistics, the original utterance is placed side by side with an equivalent (usually transcoded) in the target language. But the translator has only one side of the equation at his disposal: the source text, composed of a series of interdependent utterances." For the time being, this eminently sensible statement remains an act of defiance, as it calls into question the linguistic and comparative theories of translation.

Once it has been established that, with the exception of a few set phrases, translation equivalents are creations and that translating and transcoding are two very different activities, it becomes clear that texts (as opposed to language) multiply the linguistic means the translator has to choose from in rendering the message in the target language. This explains why translation not only is possible, but is carried out daily by translators around the world: it consists of the creation of equivalences whose "accuracy . . . is measured

by how closely the concepts match, not by the similarity or dissimilarity of
the forms in which the concepts are expressed.''

Jean Delisle uses his view of translation as a basis for developing a
teaching method designed to introduce students to the translation of pragmatic texts. As any good pedagogue must, he begins by defining course
objectives, and ensures that the exercises he proposes for limbering up novice
translators' minds for the mental gymnastics involved in grasping and
re-expressing meaning are indeed a practical application of his observations
of the translation process.

The pedagogy of translation is a difficult discipline, for it requires that
methods be found to impart not a body of knowledge but a particular skill.
Jean Delisle has met the challenge successfully.

The ideas presented in this work are those of a theorist solidly grounded
in the practice of the profession. The book contains none of the lucubra-
tions so dear to the inhabitants of the ivory tower; rather, it is the product
of experience and provides a rigorous analysis of the process of translation
(in the true sense of the word) and, thus, of the workings of language itself.

Danica Seleskovitch
Université de Paris
Sorbonne Nouvelle

Introduction

> The translation of pragmatic texts is an art
> of re-expression based on writing techniques.

This book is about the theory and teaching of translation. Its purpose is to set forth an original method for training students to translate pragmatic texts.[1] It was written for translation students, teachers of translation, and practising translators in the hope of laying to rest the notion that translation is something that cannot be taught. There are those who insist that translators, like poets, are born rather than made, and that it is impossible to inculcate the talent required for translation. While it may be true that education seeks to communicate knowledge, not impart talent, it remains to be seen whether education cannot develop the *ability* to translate, which is, after all, a skill— something that should not be confused with talent. In any case, as Henri Amiel said, talent is simply "doing with ease what others do with effort."

This book, born of ten years' reflection on translator training, is an attempt to make the teaching of translation more systematic. Having worked as a professional translator and reviser and having taught translation at the university level, I am convinced that it is possible, and even desirable, to train translators in a more methodical way and to teach more effectively— without straying into extreme dogmatism. I agree with those who think that, in a university translator-training program worthy of the name, practical instruction need not be limited to group translation exercises or correction of translated texts. Surely it is possible to design a more imaginative curriculum than that. Pedagogy is poorly served by excessive empiricism. Hastily thrown together seminars consisting of group translation and correction of

---

1. "Pragmatic" is used here as opposed to "literary." Literary texts do not have the same purpose as pragmatic texts, though some pragmatic writings resemble literature in certain respects. For a definition and justification of the term "pragmatic texts," see p. 8 and p. 16.

texts cannot help but vitiate students' motivation. The students feel, and rightly so, that they are simply marking time instead of progressing toward clearly defined goals. Without a course plan to guide them, instructors deal with translation problems randomly as they crop up in the texts. This haphazard type of instruction is not good enough. In its place we need a more methodical teaching strategy, one which is worthy of a university-level course.[2]

Some authors use the expression "translation teaching" to refer to both translator-training programs and the courses or practical seminars specifically devoted to the actual teaching of translation. It is important to distinguish clearly between the two notions. Translation programs usually include exercises in general and specialized translation; courses designed to improve language skills (grammar, vocabulary enrichment, comparative stylistics); workshops in revision and advanced writing techniques; courses in general linguistics and lexicology; and general-knowledge courses covering the institutions and economic, social, and political situations of the countries whose languages the students are translating.

The method that I describe in the following pages was specifically designed for use in practical translation courses at the introductory level. I have made no attempt to construct an ideal university program for training translators, for no matter how perfect such a program seems on paper, no program can really be universally applicable. Because the translation market is different in every country, translation programs must reflect national differences and, to a certain extent, be adapted to the particular needs of university students. Nevertheless, the general principles for introducing students to translation exercises can be applied quite widely.

Although human beings have been translating for thousands of years, they have only been teaching courses in how to translate for roughly the last forty. The increasing importance of international relations after the Second World War and the adoption of policies on official languages by bilingual nations such as Canada sparked a phenomenal growth in the volume of translation. The number of general translators has risen dramatically and in most countries far exceeds the number of literary translators. Specialized schools had to be created and training programs developed in order to quickly train these agents of communication. It is worth pointing out that these schools were not set up primarily to train literary translators, but translators of pragmatic texts.

It seems generally agreed, then, that translation can be taught as a distinct subject in its own right. However, the addition of translation to the

---

2.   This would be more than a conventional lecture course, for the classroom sessions would also usually include group discussions and practical exercises.

university calendar as an autonomous discipline has raised a number of epistemological and methodological problems that have so far defied solution. In which department, for example, does translation belong? Is it part of applied linguistics? Or is it part of psycholinguistics, semiotics, comparative literature, language learning, cognitive psychology, ethnology, or communication science? Despite the plethora of options, none has proven entirely satisfactory.

In pedagogy, efforts so far have been concentrated on curriculum content and length, admission requirements, and other general matters It is now time to expend the same effort on refining the methodology of the practical courses. Researchers seem to have largely ignored this important aspect of translation teaching, judging from the paucity of the literature.

To my knowledge, no one has really tried to answer questions such as: Is group translation or correction of texts the best way to teach what is, after all, an art of re-expression? Can we do better than simply handing out texts to translate and then correcting the students' errors? How many of their errors are attributable to a lack of method? Could translation and writing techniques be taught together? What objective criteria can be used to determine the degree of difficulty of a text for a given group of translation students, so that the instructor can teach progressively more difficult material? What difficulties do all texts of a given genre have in common? Is a real translation manual even a possibility? If more systematic instruction is desirable, how could it be structured? What basic abilities, other than linguistic, must a successful translator have? How can these abilities be developed? Are translation studies and comparative linguistics one and the same? What are the roles of the teacher and the students in a practical translation course?

These are some of the questions that must be addressed if we are going to improve the methodology of practical translation courses. Another important, but thorny, question is the problem of evaluating the quality of translations. This area of research is waiting to be explored. If we truly wish to put the era of the cobbled-together translation course behind us, we must attempt to find answers to these questions.

Having excluded the entire field of literary translation, we can consider the translator of pragmatic texts as a specialist in written communication, a language technician, or a writer. The basic premise of the translation method described in this book is that *translation is an art of re-expression based on writing techniques and a knowledge of two languages*.

Teaching someone how to translate means teaching the intellectual process by which a message is transposed into another language; that is, placing the student in the centre of the translating operation so that he can understand its dynamics. It is the *meaning* of a message that is transferred from one language to another, and the transfer is accomplished by analyzing and then reconstructing semantic relationships. This interpretation of a text—

ntxt linguistics

discourse analysis—is an act of intelligence much more demanding than the simple comparison of two linguistic systems. It requires a highly developed capacity to understand, in tandem with an ability to manipulate language.

For this reason, discourse analysis is more appropriate than traditional general linguistics for describing the act of translating.[3] A review of the current major translation theories, particularly those attempting to explain the translation process by an a posteriori examination of equivalents from two different languages, will show quite clearly that translation is not comparison. In essence, translation is re-expression of an intended meaning embodied in a text with a specific communicative function.

The model for this intellectual operation is unilingual communication. The teaching of translation should, therefore, be based on the manipulation of language rather than on the study or description of language systems. I have defined four different levels of language manipulation required in translating: (1) observing conventions of form, (2) performing interpretive analysis, (3) interpreting style, and (4) preserving textual organicity. These four levels provide a framework for classifying the basic difficulties of translation and establishing the objectives for the introductory course—in short, for organizing the course material systematically.

In an introductory course, developing skills should take precedence over imparting facts or theoretical knowledge. This should be accomplished by having students wrestle with actual translation or writing problems so that they become adept at the mental procedure involved in translation. The fundamental question in translation pedagogy—and in this book—is: How should the teaching of translation be structured so that the student emerges *mindful* of how to go about translating rather than with a *mind full* of facts?

It is often said that translation teaching should not consist in providing recipes. But just what the "recipes" are is rarely made clear. Are they practical hints? Are they ready-made solutions that can be mechanically applied to particular translation problems? Such tricks of the trade, often discovered only after many years of experience, can be a very useful complement to translator training, for they give the students a short-cut to the destination they would have reached anyway. Translation is a craft practised individually, not collectively, and outside a classroom situation it is difficult for veteran translators to pass on the fruits of their experience. Recipes are helpful, but insufficient as the basis for a systematic university-level course.

---

3.   Discourse is a unit of language higher than the sentence; it is the message taken as a whole. In this book the term "discourse" refers to written as well as spoken language. Similarly, "utterance," which in everyday usage refers mainly to speech, here covers both spoken and written language. For a discussion of the polysemy of the term "discourse," see Maingueneau, *Initiation aux méthodes d'analyse du discours*, p. 11. Discourse analysis is sometimes called text linguistics.

The systematic course I have developed has two overall objectives. The first is to provide a framework for the analysis of the linguistic and extra-linguistic contexts of a message, and the second is to encourage greater ease and flexibility in the manipulation of language in order to enhance communication. The introductory course concentrates on discovering the general principles that govern the act of translating rather than getting bogged down in the details of particular examples. It also does not waste time on arbitrarily selected problems that are not likely to recur.

The novice translator is often unable to re-express a passage, even when he understands what it means. Preoccupied with the unfamiliar forms of the original text, he has difficulty finding the corresponding words, phrases, or structures in the target language. When one is poring over a text in the source language, comprehension does not lead automatically to spontaneous re-expression, and often the search for an idiomatic and meaningful expression is unsatisfactory or even fruitless. Translators are all too familiar with the frustrations of the trial-and-error method. When a block occurs, it is a failure by thought to organize expression. Learning how to translate is, in the final analysis, learning how to think in order to communicate accurately the ideas of another person. An introductory course in translating pragmatic texts should therefore include a variety of exercises whose aim is to teach the student to re-express thoughts more easily, more accurately, and in the end, more rapidly. These exercises can be seen as a training program for the mental gymnastics of translation.

As I originally developed it in French,[4] my method included such exercises. It consisted of two parts—a basic approach to translation (an interpretive, or discourse analysis, approach with a concomitant emphasis on the manipulation of language), and pedagogical objectives and exercises that are directly related to this approach and its theoretical basis. The original French version of my book describes twenty-three pedagogical objectives and provides practical exercises enabling students to develop the specific skills needed for translating from English to French. This English version of my book is intended for a wider audience and includes only that part of my method that applies to the translation of pragmatic texts between any two languages, that is, the basic approach and its theoretical justification. The principles governing the act of translating and the four levels of language manipulation can be used to teach translation from any source language to any target language.

The second part of the method, the twenty-three objectives, is not dealt with, for many of the objectives relate specifically to differences between

---

4. *L'analyse du discours comme méthode de traduction : Initiation à la traduction française de textes pragmatiques anglais, théorie et pratique* (Ottawa: University of Ottawa Press, 1980).

English and French and the problems encountered in passing from the one language to the other. Objectives such as "French Superlative and English Comparative" and "Deixis in English: 'this,'" were inspired by characteristic differences between French and English and would be of limited use to instructors working with other languages. Some objectives, such as "Text Explication" and "Extracting Key Concepts," are more general and lend themselves to adaptation. It is my hope that teachers of translation will use the basic approach described in the first part of my method and, drawing on their intimate knowledge of their source and target languages, will develop pedagogical objectives and exercises for translation between the languages they are working with. To this end, the twenty-three objectives I defined for the introductory course in English-to-French translation are listed in Appendix 3 as a model for teachers of translation between other languages.

My aim in this book is to prove that it is both possible and necessary to identify the most important characteristics of the cognitive processes of the translation operation. I try to illustrate the complex movements involved in these mental gymnastics so as to make the teaching of translation more effective. I will start by defining the scope of the method and discussing its theoretical foundations and then move on to describe the four levels on which language is manipulated.

CHAPTER 1

Methodological Approaches

It would be difficult to imagine an introductory course in any field that did not simplify the subject matter somewhat in order to make the basic concepts easier to understand and assimilate. To simplify is to define; it is to discard what is secondary in order to penetrate to the essence of something. In the case of translation, the "subject matter" is, in fact, an intellectual process. Translation is an abstract exercise in analysis and synthesis, and cannot, therefore, be as easily divided into steps as a concrete activity can be. Its many stages overlap, and the twists and turns of thought involved in the search for equivalent concepts are difficult to follow. The translator's mind teems with ideas, images, associations, analogies, and trial solutions that he must order according to the thread of meaning he has followed through the original text so that the translation will match it point for point. Translation is a difficult activity to analyze; it owes its complexity to both the intricacy of language and the multifaceted nature of communication.

Because the process itself cannot be simplified, effective teaching of translation involves simplifying the material involved. The intellectual mechanisms of translation are the same, regardless of the nature of the text to be translated, but the professional qualifications required of the translator vary. Some texts demand that the translator master a particular register of language and have a sensitivity to the arts (for literary texts); others, that he possess specialized knowledge (for technical and scientific texts); and still others, that he be able to manipulate the spoken word (for translation for the theatre and for film dubbing). The translator is often thought of as a one-man band, and this is true up to a point, but he must respect the limits dictated by his professional conscience. Rare is the translator who can move with equal competence from literary to scientific translation, from a legal document to a medical treatise. In short, there is always a limit to the versatility of a professional translator.

To make analysis of the translation process within an introductory course simpler, the method I outline in this book applies only to pragmatic (non-literary), general (non-specialized) texts, formulated according to the rules of written (not spoken) language.

SCOPE OF THE METHOD

Source and Target Languages Used

The intellectual process of extracting meaning and reformulating it in another language is the same whatever languages are involved, because the process is no different from the functioning of language itself. At least, no one has yet demonstrated that translation between different pairs of languages requires different cognitive and memory processes. The teaching method must, however, take into account those specific differences between languages that pose problems during transposition. As Georges Mounin said: "A given translation problem is not the same between two languages *in both directions.*"[1] In other words, the interlinguistic reformulation of a message cannot be accomplished with the same linguistic tools or even the same number of words as in the original, because every linguistic community has evolved its own pattern of language customs. In this book, all the examples chosen to illustrate the processes underlying interlinguistic transfer are translations from English into French. English will be the original, or source, language, and French will be the language of the translation.[2]

Pragmatic Texts

An introductory translation course should deal with pragmatic texts, that is, texts whose fundamental purpose is to convey information and in which aesthetics are of secondary importance. Finding a clear, simple, and convenient term to cover all such texts was not easy. The expression "functional texts," modelled on expressions such as "functional language" or "functional French," would have added yet another definition to a term that already has many different meanings in science, mathematics, and everyday language. In general and applied linguistics alone, one finds not only "functional language," but also "functional linguistics," "functional education," and the "functional approach" to language teaching. However, I rejected the expression "functional texts" in favour of "pragmatic texts" largely because, in the field of language education, "functional" covers everything that is not everyday French; it applies to "apparently specific areas within

---

1.   "Un problème donné de traduction n'est pas le même entre deux langues *dans les deux sens.*" Mounin, *Les problèmes théoriques*, p. 240. (Mounin's italics)
2.   Unless otherwise indicated, English translations of quotations are our own.

the French language such as scientific, technical, and economic discourse—in short, anything that is neither literary nor 'touristic' (of the 'Where is the post office?' type)."[3] While the term "pragmatic texts" excludes literary texts, it does *not* exclude everyday language. The term "functional texts" might have been confusing. The terms "scientific texts," "technical texts," "specialized language texts," and "specialized texts" seemed too narrow and were also rejected.

Of the other solutions considered, the term "utilitarian texts" deserves mention. The problem with it is that "utilitarian" has a pejorative connotation, evident in expressions such as "purely utilitarian materialism" and "crassly utilitarian interests." According to Henri Bénac's *Dictionnaire des synonymes*, "utilitarian" is used to describe articles that are designed solely for utility at the lowest possible price and with no regard for aesthetics. "Vehicular" and "vernacular" would not do either. A "vehicular language" is a foreign tongue shared by several groups with different native languages, while a "vernacular language" is an indigenous language or dialect little used except by those for whom it is a mother tongue. Neither expression could be used to designate a category of texts. "Informative texts" was not altogether satisfactory either, because essentially, any text conveys information; the expression is tautological. Nevertheless, in this book, "informative" will sometimes be contrasted with "aesthetic" in order to emphasize the conceptual content of pragmatic messages. This is not meant to imply, however, that literary works are pure form and do not communicate anything.

There were two further reasons for choosing "pragmatic." According to the *Petit Robert*, the term applies to things that have practical applications, that are related to everyday life. Pragmatic texts generally do have a practical and immediate application. As instruments of communication, they are more or less ephemeral, at least as far as the useful life-span of their content is concerned. Seen in that light, such texts are "utilitarian," while literary texts usually exist in and of themselves, without, however, being any less necessary. Each type of text simply has a different purpose.

The second reason that weighed in favour of "pragmatic" is that it applies, in formal logic, to the use of language in actual situations of communication. While translation, as distinct from interpretation, concerns itself only with written texts and not with oral productions, it does deal with language in use (*parole* in the Saussurean sense), as does pragmatics. Syntax and semantics are concerned with language as a system (Saussure's *langue*). Some linguists do not even consider pragmatics to fall within their domain.

---

3. "domaines apparemment spécifiques à l'intérieur de la langue française : discours des sciences, des techniques, de l'économie, bref de tout ce qui n'est ni littéraire, ni 'touristique' (du type : 'Où est la poste?')." Galisson and Coste, *Dictionnaire*, at entry for "fonctionnel."

As we shall see, reflections on the theory and pedagogy of translation extend far beyond the concerns of the linguist, which for the most part are centred on syntax (the set of rules governing the combination of symbols) and semantics (the confrontation of those symbols with reality or with the symbols of another language). The translator must take into account the origin of the text to be re-expressed, its nature, and the audience for whom it was intended (its future readers). Those who study the theory or pedagogy of translation, therefore, cannot restrict themselves to the linguistic components of the text—they must draw on pragmatics in order to include in their analysis of the translation process the cognitive and situational complements that are not part of the linguistic signs.

For these two reasons—the first stemming from the nature of the texts chosen as teaching tools, the second from the theoretical foundations of the method—the term "pragmatic" seemed the most appropriate. It covers, among other things, newspaper articles, general correspondence, non-technical brochures, tourist information, and official reports and documents—in short, general texts dealing with topics like pollution, fitness, consumer affairs, drugs, leisure, economics, or sports.

Several characteristics distinguish pragmatic texts from other types of texts, such as literary or biblical texts. One is anonymity. In a pragmatic text, the focus is not on the author's impressions, as it is in a literary text, but on relatively objective facts. Pragmatic texts are therefore often anonymous, and in many cases, it would be of no use to the translator to know who wrote them. That said, it must also be recognized that the author, anonymous or not, can be a factor in how the text is interpreted. This may depend on whether he is, for example, the official spokesperson of an insurance company or the representative of aggrieved policy holders. The author of a pragmatic text is not a mere abstraction. It might sometimes be useful—or even necessary—to know who he is. For example, it might be important to know the political leanings, professional experience, and usual tone of a politically committed journalist in order to better interpret his articles. Without this knowledge, the translator might miss the journalist's allusions, innuendo, or irony. Sometimes the main point of a message is not stated explicitly. Translation is then fraught with danger, because both what is said and what is merely implied must be rendered in the target language.

The selection of texts is inevitably a subjective exercise. Because there are no objective criteria by which to accurately assess the difficulty of a text and the pace at which a group of students is progressing, the teacher must rely on his intuition and his experience as a teacher and a translator to choose the best instructional tools.[4] By going beyond the translation and correction

---

4. Difficulty of translation is both a statistical and a subjective concept (see p. 94). Translation education would benefit from research into assessing the difficulty of texts and ensuring that there is a step-by-step progression through the curriculum. In order for this to happen, translatology (see p. 28) must become experimental.

of texts chosen at random, the method proposed here partly makes up for this deficiency. The concepts considered crucial to an understanding of translation are described. This enables instructors to develop exercises that deal with the problems specific to interlinguistic transfer and combine them into a systematic teaching method that emphasizes the intellectual process involved rather than the solutions obtained.

General Texts

Student translators should not need technical or other specialized knowledge to understand the texts or parts of texts used to illustrate various aspects of the manipulation of language. An introduction to translation should not be confused with the acquisition of general knowledge. In most translation programs, courses in other disciplines cover that aspect. Although the primary purpose of a pragmatic text is to convey information, the assimilation of that information by apprentice translators is not the main object of an introductory translation course. Nor is its object to enrich students' technical vocabulary or to study systematically the concepts and phraseology of a specialized area. That is done in more advanced courses.

In order to simplify the exercise as much as possible, texts that are technical, scientific, and highly specialized are deemed to be beyond the scope of this method. In comparison with everyday language, such texts are idiosyncratic. Because of their technical content, they are difficult to translate, regardless of the translator's abilities. Although it would be a mistake to think that technical translation poses only vocabulary problems, the added difficulty of understanding the subject matter from which the specialized terminology is drawn needlessly complicates the training process, which in an introductory course should focus on the manipulation of language. *The translation process is too often blamed for problems that are due to lack of knowledge.* From a methodological point of view, it is therefore of primary importance to separate learning difficulties caused by lack of general knowledge from those having to do with the use of language per se. The countless problems arising out of deficiencies in general education must indeed be addressed in the pedagogy of translation and the design of curriculums, but not in an introductory translation course. For that matter, even the best introductory course could never make up for serious shortcomings in general knowledge: culture cannot be imparted in a single semester.

Written Texts

Unlike the interpreter, the translator essentially works with written texts. Consequently, the method outlined in this book applies to texts designed to be read, not spoken. Spoken texts are excluded because they do not conform to the same rules that govern written communication. A screenwriter, for example, is mainly concerned with producing a text that can be pronounced easily and sounds like spontaneous speech in everyday language. A translator, on the other hand, is expected to produce a text that is readable.

Speaking and writing do not take place under the same conditions. Correctness is considered more important in written language than in spoken language; written language is also more tightly constructed, more concise, and better ordered. It adheres to a rigorous syntax and obeys grammar, spelling, and punctuation rules. A good writer chooses his words carefully, avoids redundancy, and shuns awkward repetitions that make for a ponderous style. He tries to ensure that his writing is as cohesive as possible by linking ideas and sentences logically.

The translation of pragmatic texts also requires a knowledge of "codified languages" characterized by fixed expressions for which there are usually standard equivalents in the target language. Of course, for such equivalents to exist, the two languages must be closely related in terms of structure and culture, as, indeed, are English and French. Codified texts are generally cast in a standard form. The standard French equivalent of the formula "Know all by these that . . ." in a legal document is the set expression "Sachez tous par les présentes que . . . ." There are numerous examples of such equivalents in English and French; however, we will see that not all the concepts encountered in a text realized have corresponding expressions in the target language.

Some kinds of messages employ characteristic stylistic devices and syntactic structures, such as the passive voice in memorandums or instructions: "Staff members are requested to . . . ," or "It is recommended that staff members . . . ." In such standardized messages, the form, which has been chosen in the interests of clarity or uniformity, acts as a kind of mould. Drug labels, competition notices, business letters, maintenance instructions, specifications, insurance policies, and laws are all written in a form that is prescribed by tradition and easily recognizable. Certain pragmatic texts thus possess characteristics that can be identified, analyzed, and to some extent taught systematically. A method for teaching the translation of pragmatic texts must take this fact into account. A standardized text may be distinguished from one that is not standardized by the proportion of set expressions to spontaneously generated writing.

Speech, on the other hand, occurs at the speed of thought. It is typified, to varying degrees, by hesitations, superfluous words, incomplete sentences, and a limited vocabulary. The thought often develops in a meandering fashion. Sometimes what is said is awkward or incorrect by the standards of written language.[5] Singular verbs, for example, may have plural subjects. Nevertheless, the meaning of an oral discourse is perfectly clear to the listener because it fits into a situational and cognitive context. The listener supplies whatever is missing from the speech; more precisely, he follows the train of thought to its conclusion without stopping at each formal sentence boundary. Only after spontaneous speech has been written down do its structural and lexical shortcomings, in comparison with written language, become apparent. The spoken word loses much of its vigour when it is committed to paper; the pen and typewriter petrify speech. People never write exactly as they speak, nor do they speak exactly as they write. The act of writing requires one to think twice, demands a more complete maturation of one's thought. It is not merely a play on words to say that in translation the quality of this *maturation* is related to the intellectual *maturity* of the translator.

Two people conversing with each other in a real-life situation can afford to be very elliptical. A single word may be all that is necessary to conjure up a host of facts and circumstances, if both persons share the same knowledge. In written language, however, there is no context other than the linguistic one. The translator, unlike the conference interpreter who in some cases may be able to "interpret" a movement of the hand, an intonation, or a facial expression, has nothing but the text to go by. The written text is thus distinguished from the spoken word by the fact that it is more formally explicit and structured. The writer cannot always assume that his future readers will all share his knowledge. He must amplify and clarify so that all of the elements necessary for a clear understanding of his message are present. Writing is a one-way means of communication. Unintended ambiguity constitutes a failure to communicate.

---

5.   Linguists who have evaluated spoken language in terms of its grammaticality seem to have concluded that the supposedly ungrammatical nature of natural conversation should not be exaggerated: "The ungrammaticality of everyday speech appears to be a myth with no basis in actual fact. In the various empirical studies we have conducted, the great majority of utterances—about 75 percent—are well-formed sentences by any criterion. When rules of ellipsis are applied and certain universal editing rules to take care of stammering and false starts, the proportion of truly ungrammatical and ill-formed sentences fall to less than two per cent. When nonacademic speakers are talking about subjects they know well—narratives of personal experience—the proportion of sentences that need any editing at all in order to be well-formed drops to about ten percent. I have received confirmation of this general view from a great many other linguists who have worked with ordinary conversation. The myth of the ungrammaticality of spoken language seems to have two sources, data taken from the transcripts of learned conferences, where highly educated speakers are trying to express complex ideas for the first time, and the usual tendency to accept ideas that fit into our frame of reference without noticing the data with which we are surrounded." Labov, *Sociolinguistic Patterns*, p. 203.

It is worth noting that pragmatic texts are sometimes subject to space constraints—for example, in forms, catalogues, bilingual labels, and side-by-side translations. In a practical translation course, this distinctive feature can be the source of many valuable exercises.

Exclusion of Literary, or Artistic, Texts

In the interests of simplifying the translation process, all types of translation that are too idiosyncratic have been deemed to be beyond the scope of this method. Literary texts have also been ruled out. This a priori exclusion should be explained, since the vast majority of translation studies to date have dealt with what is called artistic translation. The elimination of literary texts should not be interpreted as a disparaging comment on the pedagogical value of artistic translation in a translation program. Rather, it is motivated by the methodological requirements of an introductory course. Justifying this elimination also gives me an opportunity to clarify the concept of pragmatic texts.

Characteristics of Literary Texts

Literary texts are identified by the following six criteria:

1.   In a literary work, the writer communicates *his vision of the world*, his personal perception of the reality that he has chosen to describe. Speaking always for himself, he describes *his* feelings, *his* reactions, and *his* emotions. Eugene Nida points out that "in informative communication the focus is primarily on the message, in expressive communication it is on the source," that is, the author.[6] The unity and intensity of a literary work depend on the consistency of the subjective impressions that create the work's atmosphere. In a literary work, then, the expressive function of language is predominant.

2.   An imaginative and creative work also has the *power to evoke*. Not all of the message is explicit. A large part of it remains unexpressed, hence the major role played by connotation in literature. The order of words, the rhythm of sentences, and the patterns of sound may all have an evocative power that is relevant to the message and must be conveyed by the translator. In poetry—where form plays the most important role—versification, harmony, and alliteration all reinforce the images evoked by the content. Some works even contain an entire system of symbols.

3.   In a literary work, *form is important in and of itself*. Indeed, "Art takes great pains to sheathe its content in a form that is unique, original, and aesthetic."[7] Language is not merely a means of communication, as it is in

---

6.   Nida, "A Framework for the Analysis and Evaluation of Theories of Translation," p. 48.
7.   "L'art soigne la forme pour donner une enveloppe unique, originale et esthétique à un contenu." Slama-Cazacu, *Langage et contexte*, p. 150.

pragmatic texts, it is also an end in itself. In no other type of writing are form and content so inextricable. Poetry and artistic prose seek not only to communicate, but also to elicit an emotional response. The writer uses language in a way unique to him, so that his style might even be considered a reflection of his personality. He avoids the tired cliché that betrays a lack of imagination and failure of rhetoric, and instead forges metaphors, links words in an unexpected way, and infuses fresh life into images. Form is important to the writer because his aim is to make his readers see the world in a new way.

No example better illustrates these first three characteristics of the literary text than the passage from *A Portrait of the Artist as a Young Man* in which James Joyce describes how Stephen Dedalus encounters beauty embodied in a young girl standing in a stream:

> A girl stood before him in midstream, alone and still, gazing out to sea. She seemed like one whom magic had changed into the likeness of a strange and beautiful seabird. Her long slender bare legs were delicate as a crane's and pure save where an emerald trail of seaweed had fashioned itself as a sign upon the flesh. Her thighs, fuller and softhued as ivory, were bared almost to the hips, where the white fringes of her drawers were like feathering of soft white down. Her slateblue skirts were kilted boldly about the waist and dovetailed behind her. Her bosom was a bird's, soft and slight, slight and soft as the breast of some dark plumaged dove. But her long fair hair was girlish: and girlish, and touched with the wonder of mortal beauty, her face.[8]

This scene is transfigured by symbolism. The girl is invested with all the symbolic meaning of a bird: she is "like one whom magic had changed into the likeness of a strange and beautiful seabird. Her long slender bare legs were delicate as a crane's . . . . The white fringes of her drawers were like feathering of soft white down. Her slateblue skirts were . . . dovetailed behind her." The author conveys his subjective impression (*view of the world*) of the discovery of beauty by evoking (*evocative power*) the image of the bird, which for him is synonymous with "freedom, the escape toward purity and beauty."[9] The passage is striking for its rhetorical qualities (*importance of form*). In addition to the obvious care taken with the diction and structure of the passage (Joyce describes first the girl's *legs*, then her *thighs*, her skirts kilted around the *waist*, her *bosom*, and finally her long fair *hair* and her *face*), toward the end there is an example of chiasmus ("soft and slight, slight and soft") as well as repetition and a change in the usual word order ("But her long fair hair was girlish: and girlish, and touched with the wonder of mortal beauty, her face"). A descriptive passage like this one requires

---

8. James Joyce, *A Portrait of the Artist as a Young Man* (New York: The Viking Press, 1916, 1956), p. 171. In *Comprendre et traduire*, Daniel Gouadec provides an annotated translation of this passage.
9. "[de] liberté, de départ vers la pureté et la beauté." Gouadec, *Comprendre et traduire*, p. 114.

that the translator be discerning in his choice of words, and reproduce all of the stylistic and lexical departures from the everyday language.

4.   Literary works are *not restricted to a single interpretation*. The richer a work of literature is, the more levels of meaning it contains and the more interpretations are possible. It will not mean exactly the same thing to every reader; indeed, it is almost as if the words, like the pieces of glass in a kaleidoscope, were able to assume different configurations for each reader.

5.   Literature is also characterized by a certain *timelessness*. Although it is the product and mirror of a particular era, a great literary work transcends space and time. It may be re-translated periodically, but that is to preserve its content and give new life to its form. As Keats said, "A thing of beauty is a joy forever."

6.   Lastly, a work of art stands the test of time because it is informed by *universal values*. The old works are still read today, not simply because they are aesthetically pleasing, but also because their themes have not grown stale. Love, death, religion, the human condition, the agony of existence, and relationships with others are themes for all places and all times.

I have briefly described what are, in my view, the six major distinctive traits of a work of literature. From the point of view of translation as an operation on language, the last three are of less interest than the first three. To justify excluding literary texts from an introductory translation course, I shall now examine how pragmatic texts differ from literary texts.

Characteristics of Pragmatic Texts

The further one moves away from literary texts and toward pragmatic texts, the less important subjectivity is and the more translation problems have to do with effectively conveying information. In general terms, there is a shift from more connotative language to more denotative language. According to Peter Newmark, "The basic difference between the artistic and the non-literary is that the first is symbolical or allegorical and the second representational in intention; the difference in translation is that more attention is paid to connotation and emotion in imaginative literature."[10] The literary translator, striving toward an ideal of fidelity and beauty, always seeks fresh forms of expression. The translator of informative texts aims to communicate a message accurately and effectively. Artistic communication succeeds or fails to the extent that it creates harmony between form and content and has an intellectual and emotional impact on its readers.[11] In the translation

---

10.   Newmark, "The Theory and the Craft of Translation," p. 8.

11.   Advertisements are probably the pragmatic messages most similar to literature in their attempt to play on the linguistic awareness of a given audience by clever and often humorous use of stylistic devices proper to written expression. Examples include the written form of aural puns, "L'eau Perrier, c'est l'eauptimiste"; the use of repetition, "Le cadeau qui plaît, plaît, plaît aux jeunes filles"; alliteration, "Better Because it's Bigger" (advertising a chocolate bar); and plays on well-known sayings, proverbs, or maxims, "A sprinkle a day keeps the bad odours away" (advertising a deodorant), based on "An apple a day keeps the doctor away."

of informative texts, artistic considerations are less important than clarity, aptness of expression, and conformity to the dictates of grammar and usage.

A creative work is rarely written with the needs of its readers in mind. The poet or novelist does not usually ask himself whether his readers will understand a certain word or grasp the significance of a particular image; he does not deliberate how to describe a situation so that it will be readily understood. Instead, he is alternately creator and audience, writing for himself, for he is the only reader who matters. All other readers must explore the work themselves to find what it contains. The writer of pragmatic texts proceeds completely differently, adapting what he has to say according to the nature of the message and the audience at whom it is aimed. A pragmatic text is didactic. The translator of pragmatic texts must therefore be concerned with his readers, and his approach to translation is not be the same as the literary translator's.

Some pragmatic texts do exhibit many of the stylistic qualities of a literary work. An able reporter, for example, does more than just report facts. He uses words to re-create the very atmosphere in which the events took place. Because of their style, such articles are situated at midpoint on the continuum between the purely factual (minutes of meetings, laws, instructions, chemical or medical treatises) and the artistic (novels, poems, short stories, epics). However, such stylistic qualities alone are not enough to make journalism into literature. As we saw earlier, form is only one of the elements of a creative text. Years from now, no one will re-read the accounts of the dramatic and historic meeting between Anwar Sadat and Menachem Begin carried by newspapers around the world. No one except historians, that is, for whom the accounts will provide useful information on the climate of Arab-Israeli relations at a certain point in history. Despite their polished style, these newspaper articles are pragmatic texts. Their major function is to inform, and they can do so in either a pedestrian or a lively fashion.

The following traits, then, distinguish the pragmatic text from the literary: *the pragmatic text is more denotative than connotative, it is concerned with a more or less objective reality, its primary goal is to communicate information, it generally admits of only one interpretation, it is sometimes written in a codified language, it has an immediate and short-lived use, and it tends to be didactic.*

There are also pedagogical reasons for not using works of literature in an introductory translation course. First, literary translation is an idiosyncratic genre, as are technical, scientific, and specialized translation, but for different reasons. Literary works have aesthetic qualities beyond their purely referential content. Literary language is probably the most highly refined and most difficult to translate. Because of its individualistic diction and style, it has little in common with ordinary language and writing; it tests the mettle even of experienced translators, not to mention that of students.

Second, without either minimizing the importance of the linguistic analysis involved in literary translation, or agreeing with Edmond Cary that "literary translation is not a linguistic operation but a literary one,"[12] it must be recognized that literary translation demands literary ability. It requires a sensitivity to art, born of an interest in and exposure to works of literature, which enables one to appreciate fully the feelings expressed in a work, its verbal resonance, and the symbolic import of its images. In short, it enables one to convey the artistic quality of a work. Literary translation, according to Maurice-Edgar Coindreau, is an "act of loving collaboration";[13] in other words, the translator must feel an affinity with the writer. Translating a work of literature requires more than good writing skills.

Third, it would be contrary to the principles of good teaching to base an introductory method on texts whose style is the furthest removed from that of pragmatic texts, especially when pragmatic texts constitute the overwhelming majority of a translator's work and are the very texts that have necessitated the establishment of translation schools.

Fourth, not every student entering a university translation program has mastered literary style. Experience has shown, in fact, that students' knowledge of ordinary written language and their ability to write are far from perfect. A realistic method of instruction should take this inadequacy into account.

Finally, by excluding literary texts, I define the practical translation course as training in "functional" communication and the translator as a writer who, though he does not himself put together the ideas that make up a text, is entrusted with the task of expressing them in another language. The translator thus becomes a fine craftsman, rewriting the text in a different form. By adopting this methodological stance, it is possible to emphasize two of the four major functions of language—namely, its uses as a conveyor of concepts and a tool of logical thought—and to leave aside its uses in poetry and the expression of emotions.

Because the translator of pragmatic texts need not be attuned to any one author's subjective outlook but rather takes his tone from the message itself, it seemed simpler to base the introductory course on writing techniques and business language than on an idiom as specific and idiosyncratic as poetic language.

Before setting out the theoretical foundations of my method and specifying what I mean by the manipulation of written language, I shall examine the nature of the translator's bilingualism, and determine what it is that distinguishes academic translation from professional translation.

---

12.   "La traduction littéraire n'est pas une opération linguistique [mais] une opération littéraire." Cary, "Comment faut-il traduire?" cited by Mounin, *Les problèmes théoriques*, p. 13.
13.   "acte d'amoureuse collaboration," Coindreau, *Mémoires d'un traducteur*, p. 137.

BILINGUALISM AND THE TRANSLATOR

Laymen often think that anyone who knows two languages can translate. This simplistic view explains in part the alacrity with which bilingual persons set themselves up as professional translators, assuming that they are competent when in fact they are not. The creation of translation schools throughout the world over the last forty years or so constitutes an implicit recognition that bilingualism alone is not sufficient preparation for professional translation. But how does the translator differ from a person who is bilingual in the general sense of the word, and by what criteria should his bilingualism be measured? These questions must be addressed, for their answers will guide the teaching of translation in general, and the introductory course in particular.

Bilingualism

Bilingualism is a complex and nebulous phenomenon. Any attempt to define it runs the risk of being either too broad or too narrow. Bilingualism and translation are closely related: both are products of the contact between languages that occurs when different linguistic groups communicate with each other. Unfortunately, bilingualism, like translation, cuts across many disciplines without really belonging to any of them. That is probably why bilingualism, again like translation, is still not fully understood. Psychology, sociology, linguistics, psycholinguistics, and sociolinguistics could all shed light on this multifaceted phenomenon.

The two major types of bilingualism—individual and social—have been defined in many ways.[14] The concept of individual bilingualism, which will be our primary concern here, assumes the presence of two languages in a single person. It is related to Saussure's language in use, as opposed to social bilingualism, which is related to language as a system. Most specialists define a bilingual person as one who is able to express himself in a second language. The idea of fluency in speech is implicitly linked to bilingualism, though it does not fully define it. The bilingual person is perceived, first and foremost, as one who is able to handle, with relative ease, a language other than his mother tongue. Definitions of bilingualism generally do not take into account the form of bilingualism particular to the translator, as the following examples show: "Bilingual: speaking two languages interchangeably. The ideal form of bilingualism is when both languages are spoken equally well for all purposes of life"[15] and "Bilingualism occurs when the speaker alternates between two

---

14. Beziers and Van Overbeke quote more than twenty definitions in *Le bilinguisme. Essai de définition et guide bibliographique*, and they do not claim that their list is exhaustive.
15. W. Leopold, *Speech Development*, cited in Beziers and Van Overbeke, p. 117.

languages according to his needs.''[16] According to Einar Haugen, bilingualism begins at the point where the speaker is able to make complete and meaningful statements in the other language. The bilingual person, he says, is one who can speak a second language, as opposed to one who merely understands it.[17] Jules Marouzeau has defined bilingualism as the capacity to express oneself fluently, and with equal competence, in two languages.[18] These definitions seem to confirm the commonly held opinion that only those who can speak a language actually know it.

The Translator's Bilingualism

Active knowledge of another language is not essential to the translator, but is not a drawback either.[19] Put simply, while the bilingual person generally uses his knowledge of a second language to communicate orally, the translator puts that knowledge to work for readers and writers, so that they can communicate through a written text.[20] Consequently, the translator never freely follows his own line of thought or puts forward his own ideas; nor can he express as he wishes the ideas that are given him in written form. The exposition of the author's thoughts and the ordering of the author's arguments are not his to choose. The original text imposes both qualitative and quantitative restrictions upon the translator. The qualitative restriction is that the meaning must be re-expressed, and the quantitative restriction is that the form must be respected. The translator's work is not to expound, but to reformulate. He is thus a passive bilingual who is usually not called upon to produce in his second language the message that he is translating.

   Must one be able to express oneself in a second language in order to understand it? Research on bilingualism has shown that comprehension and expression cannot be placed on an equal footing in assessing second-language knowledge, and that comprehension generally precedes and surpasses expression: ''In language, anything understood must be considered potentially expressed.''[21] Or, as another researcher has put it: ''In our native language, our ability to understand exceeds our ability to express ourselves. This is true

---

16.   ''le bilinguisme est l'usage alternatif de deux idiomes que le sujet parlant emploie tour à tour pour les besoins de son expression.'' Aurelien Sauvageot, *Problème de la structure interne et du bilinguisme*, cited in ibid., p. 119.
17.   Haugen, cited by Charbonneau-Dagenais in ''Essai de définition du bilinguisme,'' p. 34.
18.   Marouzeau, *Lexique de la terminologie linguistique français, allemand, anglais*, p. 46.
19.   The translator must often seek clarification from the author of a text that he is translating; he must then be able to speak the author's language. This, however, has to do with practising the profession and not with the actual process of translating.
20.   ''The translator's task is to re-express, to be a talking ear, a hand serving a head that is not its own.'' (''Au traducteur on demande de redire, d'être une oreille qui parle, une main au service d'une tête qui n'est pas la sienne.'') Perret, ''Traduction et parole,'' p. 14.
21.   ''En matière de langues, il faut considérer toute compréhension comme une expression virtuelle.'' Beziers and Van Overbeke, *Le bilinguisme*, p. 105.

of speech and even more true of writing."[22] The bilingual person is thus able to express himself fully in his second language, while the translator needs only to understand it. The translator need not be a true bilingual as defined by Christopher Thiery,[23] because translation consists in "SAYING [or rather writing] WELL, IN A LANGUAGE THAT ONE KNOWS VERY WELL, WHAT ONE HAS UNDERSTOOD VERY WELL IN A LANGUAGE THAT ONE KNOWS WELL."[24] The translator can thus dispense with an oral knowledge of the language of the original message, as long as he fully understands it in its written form. Because the translator essentially deals with written text, the ability to speak a second language fluently is superfluous. Nevertheless, people who know a language perfectly without having lived in the country where it is spoken are few and far between.

The translator's bilingualism is characterized, above all, by the ability to preserve the integrity of two languages in contact. Translation is the ultimate case of language contact, one "in which the resistance to the usual consequences of bilingualism is the most deliberate and methodical, the case in which the bilingual speaker consciously battles against any lapse from correct language and any interference."[25] In evaluating the bilingualism of the translator, it is irrelevant to measure the extent of his vocabulary or his knowledge of grammar and spelling and even less appropriate to measure his fluency in the second language. It is the translator's ability not to confuse two languages in contact that indicates his knowledge of those languages and his mastery of his profession, and thus distinguishes him from the bilingual person in the usual sense of the word.

Tracing the route from conceptualization to expression is not easy. It seems that ideally—for there are various degrees of bilingualism—the balanced bilingual, who expresses himself spontaneously in his second language, does not translate. He does not compose his message in one language and then transpose it into another. Such spontaneous expression is what language teachers try to inculcate in their students by teaching them

---

22. "En langue maternelle, nos capacités de compréhension dépassent nos capacités d'expression. Cette constatation faite à propos de l'oral, est encore plus vraie dans l'ordre scriptural." Moirand, "Approche globale des textes écrits," p. 88.
23. "An individual can be said to be truly bilingual when members of socioculturally equivalent milieus within the two linguistic communities to which he belongs each take him to be one of their own." (True bilingualism is "le fait pour un individu d'être pris pour un des leurs par les membres de milieux socio-culturels équivalents de chacune des deux communautés linguistiques auxquelles il appartient.") Thiery, *Le bilinguisme chez les interprètes de conférence professionnels*, p. 8.
24. "DIRE BIEN [par écrit] DANS UNE LANGUE QU'ON SAIT TRÈS BIEN, CE QU'ON A TRÈS BIEN COMPRIS DANS UNE LANGUE QU'ON SAIT BIEN." Grandjouan, *Les linguicides*, p. 227 (upper case in the original).
25. ". . . où la résistance aux conséquences habituelles du bilinguisme est la plus consciente et la plus organisée; le cas où le lecteur bilingue lutte consciemment contre toute déviation de la norme linguistique, contre toute interférence." Mounin, *Les problèmes théoriques*, p. 5.

to "think" directly in a second language. In reality, they are trying to get the students used to "formulating their thoughts" in a second language, or short-circuiting their first language.[26] Normally a bilingual person does not refer to a signifier and signified[27] in his native language in order to arrive at a signifier and signified in his second language. He uses different means of expression for each language and he accesses them directly.

In the act of translation, on the other hand, concepts are necessarily apprehended through the signifier/signified of the original language—the very nature of translation requires it. The relationships between concepts and speech in the bilingual person and the translator are represented in simplified fashion in Figure 1.

Figure 1

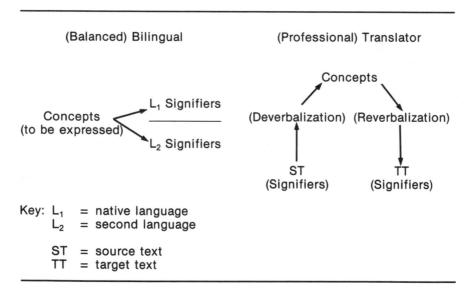

(Balanced) Bilingual   (Professional) Translator

Concepts (to be expressed) → L₁ Signifiers / L₂ Signifiers

Concepts

(Deverbalization) (Reverbalization)

ST (Signifiers)   TT (Signifiers)

Key: L₁ = native language
     L₂ = second language

     ST = source text
     TT = target text

Since spontaneous expression is not possible in written texts, the translator's bilingualism is inevitably "deliberate and methodical." This is one reason why translation is a skill that demands an apprenticeship, even of

---

26. The structures of thought are not moulded by linguistic structures; if they were, bilingualism and translation would be impossible. Hence the necessity of inserting a non-verbal conceptualization stage between thought and speech. See Buyssens, "Le langage et la logique—Le langage et la pensée," pp. 76-90, and Seleskovitch, *Langage, langues et mémoire*. Also see chapter 2 below, "Analysis of the Translation Process," and Figures 3 and 4.

27. "Signifier" (*signifiant*) and "signified" (*signifié*) are terms used by the Swiss linguist Ferdinand de Saussure (1857-1913) to describe the two aspects of the linguistic sign (see p. 42, "Translation and Transcoding").

a person who is truly bilingual.[28] The rapidity and ease with which the novice translator learns to free himself from the form of the original depends on his talent. Some people readily describe themselves, with more than a touch of vanity, as "perfectly bilingual." Almost no one describes himself as "perfectly unilingual," for fear of seeming conceited. And yet, is that not exactly what is required of the translator—the most thorough knowledge possible of his mother tongue? Is it not primarily the quality of the target language that is judged? Teachers of translation can attest that their best students are not always the so-called perfect bilinguals. Hilaire Belloc even wondered "whether a bilingual person has ever been known to make a good translation."[29]

The Apprentice Translator

It is fairly easy to pinpoint the cause of many of the errors made by novice translators. They are so blinded by the strange forms of the second language that they do not analyze the context closely enough and, as a result, interpret the message incorrectly or incompletely. Their translations slavishly follow the words and structures of the original text. This tendency could be explained by the fact that "the mental effort required to produce a literal translation is far less than that required to think a translation through intelligently."[30] The foreign signs of the original text interfere with spontaneous re-expression by the bilingual person who is inexperienced in the mental gymnastics of transfer between languages. The beginner in a translation program finds himself in a situation comparable to that of a student starting to learn a foreign language. Both must become accustomed to freeing themselves from the influence of another language—the translator, from the forms of the source language, and the language student, from the forms of his mother tongue. Both must learn not to equate the surface structures of one language with those of another.

The nature of the introductory translation course is directly influenced by this aspect of the translator's bilingualism. The general objective of the course will be to overcome the masking effect of the original text by providing the novice translator with a rigorous analytical method for finding the best way of rendering the author's intention. The translator works indirectly with the source language and directly with the target language. Therefore, the bilin-

---

28. "Facility in translation is not easily come by . . . . Even a bilingual may find it difficult to translate if he has not previously been trained for it." Kirstein, "Reducing Negative Transfer," p. 78. George Steiner expressed a similar opinion in *After Babel*, p. 119.
29. Belloc, "On Translation," p. 38.
30. "L'effort mental exigé par une traduction littérale est bien moindre que celui qu'impose une traduction réfléchie." Seleskovitch, *Langage, langues et mémoire*, p. 56.

gualism of the translator is characterized by passive comprehension of the source language, active knowledge of the written forms of the target language, and the ability to discern the meaning of a text. According to Peter Newmark, "Any old fool can learn a language, if he has enough determination to do so, but it takes an intelligent person to become a translator, and basically his work is the measure of his intelligence."[31] The precise nature of the act of translating (which is based on the manipulation of language) and the problems it poses for beginning translators will become clearer if we compare the translation process with that of spontaneous speech in the unilingual or balanced bilingual person.

In spontaneous speech, meaning is associated more or less unconsciously with the linguistic signs that carry it. The signs transmit meaning as the speaker produces them. The hearer apprehends the meaning of the words as he perceives them. In verbal communication, the movement from language system to language use is unconscious and instantaneous. Only occasionally does the speaker "search for words." Here the expression "searching for words" could be seen as a euphemism for "searching for ideas," for when an idea is clearly conceived, the words to express it come easily. (This statement would not apply to non-verbal types of intelligence or to people who are not used to expressing their thoughts verbally. However, such people do not usually become translators.)

Thoughts contained in a text are a different matter. Already embodied in linguistic signs, they have been translated once simply by being transcribed. Rather than springing from an oral, invisible, and fleeting base, as in a speech act, the significations rest upon a written, visible, and enduring foundation. Confronted by ideas already set down in writing, the translator naturally has a tendency to be distracted by the signs of the foreign language as he searches for conceptual equivalents. He is easily tempted to assign the wrong content to a given form. This leads to semantic distortion in the target language as the source language leaves its mark on the translated text. Unlike the speaker who is spontaneously expressing himself in his mother tongue, the translator must remain ever vigilant lest he succumb to lexical or other forms of interference.

The process of translating is semasiological and onomasiological. Indeed, translation consists of mentally dissociating a concept from its written form in order to match signs drawn from a different linguistic system with it. Ideas, therefore, cannot be expressed until after they have been grasped, whereas in spontaneous speech, concepts are unconsciously and more or less immediately connected with linguistic signs. That is why texts are not translated at the speed at which they are read or heard. Translation involves two stages of reflection. Whether it is more intellectually demanding to re-express

---

31.   Newmark, "Some Notes on Translation," p. 85.

thoughts that another has already put down on paper, or to articulate one's own ideas, is a moot point.

In short, we are dealing with two different forms of bilingualism—the oral fluency of the bilingual person (associated with spontaneous speech acts) and the translator's command of written language—which bear little relation to each other. While the former has learned to use a second language, the latter has acquired a passive knowledge of one. Insofar as the mother tongue is concerned, translators are similar to writers in that both must respect the same strict rules of composition. We shall return to that later; let us now consider whether language instruction as such can form the basis of a translation course and contribute to developing the type of bilingualism peculiar to the translator. We must also ask ourselves whether the pedagogy of translation and pedagogical translation are one and the same thing.

ACADEMIC TRANSLATION AND PROFESSIONAL TRANSLATION

One has only to skim the calendars of translation schools to realize that command of at least two languages is always a requirement for admission. Surely this indicates that knowledge of languages is a *prerequisite* for training in translation or practising it as a profession. The importance of this knowledge must not be underestimated as it was by a somewhat unenlightened character of Diderot's, who said that one need not understand a language in order to translate it because one only translates for those who do not understand.[32]

Translating begins and ends with language. The better the translator's command of the languages involved, the slighter the chance of misunderstanding or interference in the reformulation of the meaning of a message. It is therefore normal and even desirable that courses in both the mother tongue and the second language figure prominently in translation programs. It would, however, be a mistake to think that translation teaching can be reduced to the acquisition of linguistic knowledge or to the educational exercises used in language teaching.

In order to set specific goals for the introductory course, we must clearly differentiate between professional translation and academic translation.[33] I will not, however, pass judgement on the respective worth of the various methods currently used in language teaching (grammar-translation, direct, audio-oral, audio-visual); nor will I contribute to the controversy over the appropriateness of translation exercises for language learning.

---

32. Denis Diderot, *Les Bijoux indiscrets* (Paris : Garnier-Flammarion, 1968), p. 225.
33. The distinction must be drawn in order to counter the belief, still current in some circles, that translation teaching covers the same ground as language teaching. This is a simplistic and erroneous notion that must be refuted. We shall see that the basic orientation of translation teaching, or at least of practical training in the field, differs from that of language teaching.

Academic Translation

Academic, or pedagogical, translation is intended to help the student acquire the rudiments of a language or, at a more advanced level, to perfect his style. It is never an end in itself, but always a means. According to Edmond Cary, "Translation serves teaching, but is not served by it."[34] Indeed, to avoid ambiguity, it would be better to use the French terms *thème* and *version* in this context, since they refer specifically to translation as an academic exercise.[35]

As taught in school, *version* is above all an exercise in style. It also tests comprehension of the second language, as measured by the number of mistranslations, shifts in meaning, and absurdities. *Thème*, as practised in the early stages of language learning, is designed to implant the structures of the second language in the student's mind; at that elementary level, it is more a grammar exercise than translation per se. At the intermediate level, *thème* can be used to expand vocabulary or emphasize points of morphology and syntax. Elementary and intermediate exercises in *thème* and *version* are not generally based on a message with any real communicative value, but on linguistic forms; they are exercises in transcoding (see "Translation and Transcoding"). Who could forget the classic phrases—"This is a pencil"; "The book is red"; "My name is John"—with which the student is introduced to a different way of putting thoughts into words, or the lists of isolated terms to be "translated"? This "translation" is akin to a recodification of the mother tongue using the signs of a foreign language not yet mastered. Finally, at a much more advanced stage, exercises in literary translation are used to enhance the student's ability to express himself in a foreign language. *Thème* then, is little more than "*version* backwards," as Jean-René Ladmiral puts it.

Professional Translation

The teacher of translation pursues different goals. He does not aim to implant the structures of a foreign tongue, improve his students' command of a language (native or foreign), or even perfect their style. Ladmiral points out: "Translation in the true sense is a performance in itself, while academic translation is merely a test of performance."[36] The professional translator does not translate words or sentences in the abstract, but real texts aimed

---

34. "L'enseignement se sert de la traduction, il ne la sert pas." Cary, *La traduction dans le monde moderne*, p. 167.
35. Ladmiral, "La traduction," p. 17.
36. "La traduction proprement dite vise à la production d'une performance pour elle-même, [tandis que] la traduction pédagogique est seulement un test de performance." Ladmiral, "La traduction," p. 18.

at specific audiences. These messages have a context and are subject to many constraints, imposed not by an educational institution but by the writer, the nature of the text, and the intended audience. Professional translation demands that the translator understand the text before beginning his work, since its very point is to make a text understood, not to test comprehension, as is the case when translation is used in language instruction. True translation must overcome all the difficulties a message presents, because that message carries precise information. That is why " 'free translation,' or translation that replaces the statement in its entirety with another statement that stands in the same relation to the situation in its entirety, is the only form of translation worthy of the name."[37] Functionally defined, translation has communication as its objective.

It would be a mistake to confuse the goals of academic translation with those of professional translation. Because the purpose of professional translation is to transmit the meaning of a text, translation training is designed to teach the student to manipulate language so that he can make it carry a given meaning in a given situation. As a process of interpretation and communication, translating transcends language. From a linguistic point of view, assimilating a foreign language is a matter of internalizing a set of rules and a lexicon, while translating a message is an attempt to achieve perfect identity of meaning by pairing one language's concepts with another's. To learn a foreign language is to acquire an extra tool of communication; to translate a text is to perform an act of communication. Subtle though this distinction may seem, it is of paramount importance to the teaching of translation. The translator defines himself first and foremost as a communicator.

Translation requires an adroit command of the resources of the target language. Therefore, finding the means of expression with which to match concepts is certainly not incompatible with the goals of the introductory course. Adding to the student translator's expressive palette ("expressive" in the sense of "capable of expressing himself so as to be understood") could even be considered an important objective of the course. Knowing *how to put it* (using writing techniques) is a significant aspect of the *know-how* of translation. The epigraph at the beginning of this book underlines the importance of writing techniques in my methodology.

Qualities of the Translator

Many attempts have been made to identify the innate qualities of the professional translator. An aptitude for analysis and synthesis, an interest in

---

37. "Seule, en fait, mérite le nom de traduction . . . la 'traduction libre', c'est-à-dire celle qui remplace la totalité d'un énoncé par un autre énoncé présentant les mêmes caractéristiques d'adéquation à la totalité de la situation." Pergnier, "Traduction et théorie linguistique," p. 37.

language and a taste for working alone, a capacity for concentration, an ability to work in a methodical and disciplined fashion, wide-ranging curiosity, intellectual maturity, a keen critical sense, and sound judgement generally head the list. All these qualities are certainly desirable in a translator, but they are not specific to the profession of translation. Surely the historian, linguist, biologist, and physician must also display a high degree of intellectual curiosity, be adept at analysis and synthesis, possess sound judgement, and go about their work methodically. Whatever qualities one chooses to include in the psychological profile of the translator, they are likely to be of value in many other disciplines as well.

For the purposes of teaching translation, it is more useful to determine whether the student's mastery of certain fundamental aspects of the cognitive processes involved in translation—such as drawing analogies, interpreting the meaning of a text through analysis and logical reasoning, discerning the underlying structure of a text, and others, which will be considered in chapters 2 and 3—could be developed by some means other than the manipulation of language. Apart from strictly linguistic exercises, which in many cases cannot be replaced, could other indirect methods of improving the reasoning and analytical capacity of future translators be devised? Surely every text has its own logic? Can it be understood except by a chain of reasoning? There is no reason to believe that exercises in logic would not be a very beneficial form of mental gymnastics for student translators. It will be the business of applied translatology[38]—still in its infancy—to assess the real usefulness of paralinguistic training methods. This whole area remains to be researched.

The point I have sought to make in expounding upon academic and professional translation and the qualities of the translator is that pedagogical translation cannot be equated with the pedagogy of translation. Schools of translation are not language learning centres; they define the translator as a *language technician* because *translating is an intellectual process that consists in re-articulating a thought expressed in a context.* Just as knowing how to write is not enough to make one a writer, knowing two languages is not enough to make one a translator. Linguistic competence is a necessary but not sufficient condition for the practice of translation as a profession.

---

38.   This term, coined by Brian Harris, seems to have been accepted as a label for the science of translation, or at least for its systematic study. See Harris's "La traductologie," pp. 134-135, and "Toward a Science of Translation," pp. 90-92. The new term, whose French equivalent is "traductologie," was taken up by Gerardo Vázquez-Ayora, the author of *Introducción a la traductología.*

CONCLUSION

In this chapter I have outlined an approach to the teaching of translation. For methodological and pedagogical reasons, my course in the translation of pragmatic texts focuses on the cognitive processes of interlinguistic transfer, rather than examining the structural differences between two idioms. Very idiosyncratic types of translation are excluded in order to simplify the material. The particularities—highly specialized content, spoken language, an added aesthetic dimension—of certain types of texts might have obscured the basic operations involved in the process and made it more difficult to analyze.

This methodological stance is justified by the lack of any generally applicable minimum standard of professional competence in translation. Since it was impossible to teach Translation with a capital "T," I had to decide what type of text would be best suited to imparting the technique, without losing sight of the overall goals of university training programs. Furthermore, a course in literary translation would not be structured in the same way as one in legal, technical, commercial, or advertising translation. The pedagogical aims would be different in each case. If the debate on translation teaching is to be couched in specific terms, we shall have to identify the idiosyncrasies of each broad category of texts to be translated, for each category requires a particular methodology. In order for professional translation to be taught effectively, the debate must be broken down in this way.

A sense of the general approach to be taken in the introductory course has emerged from my definition of the translator's bilingualism. A text makes thoughts concrete by putting them into words; in itself it poses an obstacle which student translators, easily seduced by the foreign idiom, find difficult to surmount. The balanced bilingual expressing himself spontaneously in speech has no such hurdle to overcome. Marianne Lederer has said that "The foreign language [is] an obstacle to be overcome rather than an object to be translated."[39] I shall take this point up again in the next chapter.

It has not been difficult to show that academic translation and professional translation have little in common. They serve different purposes: the former is a step in language learning, while the latter is part of a process of communication. Academic translation thus *precedes* professional translation. It follows that the methodological design of the introductory course must be based on the precise nature and purpose of professional translation, not of academic translation. Matching concepts and reformulating a message

---

39. "La langue étrangère [est] un obstacle à surmonter plutôt qu'un objet à traduire." Lederer, "Synecdoque et traduction," p. 39.

in order to communicate something is not the same as learning a foreign language and assimilating the culture underlying it.

All structured teaching strategies are based on theoretical models that provide frames of reference and ensure coherence and unity. It is appropriate at this point to examine the theoretical foundations of my methodology. Many theoretical models have been put forth to explain translation. There are semiotic, linguistic, sociolinguistic, comparative, and interpretive approaches, all of which, by disparate and sometimes divergent routes, seek to account for the different linguistic, cultural, and psychological aspects of the act of establishing translation equivalences.

In the next chapter, after a brief analysis of the major theories, I will define two types of equivalents, "transcoded" and "contextual." Much of the confusion and many of the erroneous ideas encountered in the fields of translation theory and pedagogy arise from the fact that not enough importance has been attached to the distinction between these two types of equivalents. The analysis of language is very different from the analysis of discourse. Translating a text is completely different from translating isolated segments of language.

CHAPTER 2

Theoretical Foundations of the Method

It is no more necessary to have a knowledge of the theories of translation in order to translate than it is to have a knowledge of the rules of language in order to speak. Good translators have always intuitively applied the rules of functional equivalence without having had to learn the "scientific" laws of translation. However, once it is no longer a matter of translating but of teaching someone else how to translate, the limitations of an empirical approach become obvious. If teaching is to be effective, it must be based on a sound and coherent body of rules that, though not absolute, will provide a framework for learning to perform a complex intellectual activity.[1]

There will always be translators who have the ability to transpose messages from one language to another without consciously referring to a set of principles. Today, however, the ever increasing demand for professional translators cannot be met by the few individuals who are able to dispense with systematic training. There are also translators whose work is unsatisfactory because they have not devoted any thought to the problems of translation, and others who are convinced that language rather than meaning must be translated. Dilettante translators have generally been replaced by "mercenary" ones, who usually require a training period before they can join the ranks of professional translators. In most cases, intuitive knowledge of the rules of translation is not enough. It is not by chance that the most important work in translation theory has coincided with the dramatic increase in the volume of pragmatic texts translated around the world, and the establishment of professional schools of translation. Teaching requires the systematization of empirical knowledge because, before a phenomenon can be explained, it must be broken down into its constituent parts.

---

1. "Any discussion of translation presupposes a theory of language. It is only at this level that the practical problems crystallize and become intelligible; it is only at this level that the doctrines on the art of translation can be compared and appraised." ("Tout discours sur la traduction suppose une théorie du langage. C'est seulement à ce niveau que les problèmes pratiques trouvent consistance et intelligibilité; c'est seulement à ce niveau que les doctrines relatives à l'art de traduire peuvent être comparées et appréciées.") Perret, "Traduction et parole," p. 9.

THEORIES OF TRANSLATION

Until the Second World War, theories of translation were almost always philological comparisons of texts, and criteria for judging the fidelity of a translation were philosophical, aesthetic, or social, depending on the age. The observations made were often valid, but they were scattered among a great many heterogeneous general impressions or subjective intuitions, and essentially had to do with how the great writers should be translated. The proposed methods of translating varied with the changing tastes of readers.[2] Theodore H. Savory had in mind this mass of disparate and sometimes contradictory observations handed down by literary translators through the ages when he said:

> a statement of the principles of translation in succinct form is impossible, and . . . a statement in any form is more difficult than might be imagined; and further, . . . this difficulty has arisen from the writings of the translators themselves. The truth is that there are no universally accepted principles of translation, because the only people who are qualified to formulate them have never agreed among themselves, but have so often and for so long contradicted each other that they have bequeathed to us a volume of confused thought which must be hard to parallel in other fields of literature.[3]

The literary translators never learned to use their experience as a basis for constructing theories; they sought to justify their personal notions of translation as an art, instead of studying translation as a practice in order to identify theoretical hypotheses and general principles and rules. In this sense, their approach was not scientific.

In the fifties, theoretical studies that departed from the previous reflective works began to appear. These works integrate the advances made in linguistics and other disciplines, of which psychology, sociology, and ethnology are the most important, and are more scientific, or at least more systematic, in their approach. Generally, they are more descriptive than prescriptive. Subjective impressions and value judgements are emphasized much less than before. These works attempt to explain the phenomenon of translation, although by different means and with varied success. The best of them try to elucidate the relationships between language and thought. These changes show that translation scholars were defining both their field of investigation and their methods more closely.

The most important and original research in non-literary translation carried out in the last thirty years includes (in chronological order) *Stylis-*

---

2. See the historical retrospectives by Ljudskanov, *Traduction humaine*, vol. 1, pp. 18-29; Kelly, *The True Interpreter*; and Mounin, *Les belles infidèles*.
3. Savory, *The Art of Translation*, pp. 49-50.

tique comparée du français et de l'anglais (1958) by Jean-Paul Vinay and Jean Darbelnet, *Toward a Science of Translating* (1964) by Eugene A. Nida and *The Theory and Practice of Translation* (1969) by Eugene A. Nida and Charles Taber, *A Linguistic Theory of Translation* (1965) by John C. Catford, and *Traduction humaine et traduction mécanique* (1969) by Alexander Ljudskanov. *Les problèmes théoriques de la traduction* (1963) by Georges Mounin should also be mentioned, although, despite its title, it is not really a work on translation theory. Rather, the book explores "all the modern linguistic theories in order to determine whether, by completely destroying confidence in our ability to deal intelligently with the meaning of linguistic utterances, they impugn the legitimacy of translation."[4]

One other theoretical study, whose approach is philosophical, has received no notice at all, but is worthy of mention. This is an unpublished thesis by Stanley N. Weissman, "Foundations of a Theory of Translation for Natural Languages." In his preface, Weissman says:

> The present study is an attempt to formulate and defend a philosophical theory of translation for natural languages. So that no reader may be misled about what he may expect here, it is important to stress the words "philosophical theory." It is not a manual of advice for translators, but is rather aimed at understanding translation, at identifying the features which distinguish translations from other sorts of things, and at describing some of the components relevant to evaluating translations. . . . In the first chapter, two distinguished treatments of translation, in the context of logical systems, are examined. . . . The second chapter provides a transition between logical systems and natural languages, by providing a glimpse into the ways in which linguists have recently understood their subject matter. . . . The third chapter is devoted to identifying some of the major components in a measure for degree of translation. . . . The fourth chapter considers how the identified components [syntactic or grammatical] can be utilized in the explication of "degree of translation." [In] the concluding chapter . . . we try to show that translation has a special role in the evaluation of philosophical theories.[5]

To this list of works on translation theory should be added those of the research group at the École Supérieure d'Interprètes et de Traducteurs (Sorbonne Nouvelle, Paris III). The innovative contribution of these works is that they lay the foundations of an "interpretive" theory of translation. They demonstrate that a true theory of translation must be co-extensive with a general theory of discourse and therefore cannot be a simple extension of a purely linguistic theory describing language as a system. As opposed to

---

4. ". . . toutes les théories linguistiques modernes afin de vérifier si, détruisant toute confiance dans notre aptitude à traiter intelligemment du sens des énoncés linguistiques, elles atteignent la légitimité de la traduction." Mounin, *Les problèmes théoriques*, p. 35.
5. Weissman, "Foundations," pp. ii-vii.

the linguistic theories of translation, the Paris School offers an approach based on the analysis of the meaning of discourse.

Among the works published by members of the school are, in chronological order, *L'interprète dans les conférences internationales* (1968) by Danica Seleskovitch; *Exégèse et traduction* (1973); *Langage, langues et mémoire* (1975) by Danica Seleskovitch; *Traduire : les idées et les mots* (1976); *Lectures et improvisations : Incidences de la forme de l'énonciation sur la traduction simultanée (français-allemand)* (1978) by Karla Dejean Le Féal; *Les déviations délibérées de la littéralité en interprétation de conférence* (1978) by Mariano Garcia-Landa; *Les fondements sociolinguistiques de la traduction* (1978) by Maurice Pergnier; *La traduction simultanée, fondements théoriques* (1980) by Marianne Lederer; *Interpréter pour traduire* (1984) by Danica Seleskovitch and Marianne Lederer; *Décomposition de la démarche propre à la traduction technique en vue de dégager les principes pour une pédagogie de la traduction* (1984) by Christine Durieux; and *Traduction technique et pédagogie* (1986) by Monique C. Cormier. The present work, *Translation: An Interpretive Approach*, first published in French in 1980, is rooted squarely in the theory of meaning espoused by the École Supérieure d'Interprètes et de Traducteurs in Paris.

It is perhaps misleading to use the word "theory" for most of the works just mentioned, even though their aim is to explain the phenomenon of translation and identify the principles underlying the intellectual process. According to James S. Holmes, a true theory is "a series of statements, each of which is derived logically from a previous statement or from an axiom and which together have a strong power of explanation and prediction regarding a certain phenomenon." He goes on to say:

> Most of the theoretical presentations that we have had until now, although they have called themselves theories, are not really theories in the strict sense. They have an air of unclear thinking about the problems before them without the strict logical development of a theory.[6]

It is not within the scope of this book to undertake a detailed critical analysis of each of these attempts to analyze translation systematically. Nevertheless, some general observations must be made in order to clearly establish the theoretical foundations of the method proposed here. First, it must be noted that not all theorists approach the theory of translation pragmatically, in terms of its application to teaching, as I do. Nor do they all agree on what the objectives of a theory of translation should be. Some think, for example, that their role is not to develop rules or recipes for translators, "but to make systematic what is most general in the work of

---

6. Holmes, "Translation Theory," pp. 56-57.

the translator, to extract from it those elements that lend themselves to analysis. . . ."[7] However, Jean-Paul Vinay, who specializes in comparative stylistics, argues that "the primary purpose of a satisfactory [translation theory] is to make translation easier," and to generate practical rules.[8] I will first consider the objectives set by Alexander Ljudskanov, John C. Catford, and Eugene A. Nida. I will examine the comparative method of Jean-Paul Vinay and Jean Darbelnet in detail once I have broken down the cognitive process of translation into its components.

Semiotic Theory [9]

The semiotician Alexander Ljudskanov views translation as a special case of the automation of human creative activities and focuses his research on the mathematical formalization of the translator's activity. The main problem he seeks to solve is "how to formalize extra-linguistic analysis and 'transform' an analysis based on signifieds into a formal linguistic analysis."[10] Thus, the goal of this theory is to describe the activity of the translator mathematically, or scientifically. Ljudskanov believes that this formal description could apply to humans as well as machines, and should help "illuminate the

---

7. "mais de systématiser ce qu'il y a de plus général dans le travail du traducteur, de dégager de l'expérience les aspects qui se prêtent à l'analyse. . . ." Etkind, "La stylistique comparée," p. 23. Ladmiral offers a similar opinion: "what may be expected of a theory of translation is . . . assistance in *conceptualizing*, formulating and posing as problems the difficulties that a translator encounters in his work; this assistance cannot consist of what are sometimes erroneously called 'translation techniques', which may be deduced linearly from a true or 'scientific' theory." ("Ce qu'il est permis d'attendre d'une théorie de la traduction, c'est . . . une aide à la *conceptualisation*, à la problématisation et à la formulation des difficultés que rencontre le traducteur dans son travail : cela ne peut pas être ce qu'on appelle parfois à tort des 'techniques de traduction,' qui puissent être déduites de façon linéaire à partir de la théorie vraie ou 'scientifique'." *Traduire : théorèmes pour la traduction*, p. 116.
8. "la principale raison d'être d'une [théorie de la traduction] adéquate est de faciliter l'acte de traduction." Vinay, "Regards sur l'évolution des théories," p. 17.
9. Linguistics is the scientific study of language; semiotics, according to some of its modern practitioners (including the late Alexander Ljudskanov), is the study of all the sign systems used in a society: dress, rituals and customs, algebra, various codes (highway code, Morse code, and so on), signals, musical notation, natural languages. For Saussure, semiology and semiotics were synonyms, but for Mounin, the use of semiology is limited to the study of sign systems other than natural languages. There is no clear dividing line between semiotics and semiology. Opinions differ also as to whether semiotics is part of linguistics, or vice versa. "Given [the] necessity of approaching semiology through linguistics and the relative meagreness of sign systems other than language, it would seem more appropriate today to consider semiology a branch of linguistics rather than the reverse." ("Compte tenu de [la] nécessité de passer par la linguistique pour aborder le sémiologique et de la relative pauvreté des systèmes de signes autres que la langue, on aurait plutôt tendance aujourd'hui à considérer la sémiologie comme une branche de la linguistique et non le contraire.") Galisson and Coste, *Dictionnaire*, at entry for "sémiologie."
10. ". . . formalisation de l'analyse extra-linguistique et la 'transformation' de l'analyse linguistique basée sur les côtés signifiés en analyse linguistique formelle." Ljudskanov, *Traduction humaine*, vol. 2, p. 58.

relationships between human thought and language."[11] The theory has four specific objectives: (1) to analyze thoroughly the structure of languages, (2) to describe these structures by means of algorithms,[12] (3) to establish correspondences between languages, and (4) to create multilingual algorithms for machine translation. The overall objective of his program is to develop a general model of translation as part of a scientific theory of semiotic transformations.

For the semiotician, language is only one of many codes. The concept of translation, therefore, transcends natural languages. Viewed as a cybernetic process, translation includes all transformations of signs: it can be carried out between two natural languages, a natural language and an artificial one, or even between two artificial languages. Based on the premise that "translation, like all forms of communication, is semiotic in nature and amounts to a transformation of signs,"[13] this ambitious theory rigorously analyzes the basic mechanisms underlying translation and raises many metatheoretical questions.

In a creative process it is not possible to transfer signs without first analyzing the information they carry and also drawing on the supplementary information that is necessary to interpret them correctly. This "supplementary information" corresponds to the "cognitive complements" of the interpretive theory of translation being developed by the Paris School (see pp. 59 and 67). It is hard to imagine the complex algorithms that would be necessary to formalize the affective impact of the words of a text, the emotional and aesthetic qualities of a work of literature, or the linguistic sensitivity of a people during a given era. Without such algorithms, there would be no guarantee that the decoding of an original message and its recoding in the symbols of another linguistic code would transfer the original intention of the author to the receiver in its entirety. Clearly, then, translation essentially takes place in the area lying between two linguistic codes.

It is difficult to reconcile the objectives of this theory, which in a sense aspires to become the theory of translation theories, with the immediate and concrete goals of the translation teacher. The purpose of teaching "human" translation is to equip the novice translator to make linguistic choices in the process of postulating an equivalence. Semiotic theory is highly abstract. It

---

11.   ". . . lever le rideau qui cache le mécanisme des rapports entre la pensée humaine et la langue." Ljudskanov, "À propos des *Problèmes théoriques de la traduction*," *T.A. Informations*, p. 111.
12.   An algorithm is a series of basic operations used to perform a calculation or solve a particular class of problems. Grammar may be considered an algorithm in linguistics just as formulas are in mathematics.
13.   "L'opération traduisante, de même que toutes les formes de la réalisation de la communication ont une nature sémiotique et reviennent à des transformations de signes." Ljudskanov, *Traduction humaine*, vol. 2, p. 41.

has not yet been developed sufficiently to provide a body of concrete principles or rules substantial enough to serve as an organizational framework for teaching the translation of pragmatic texts, particularly since it is basically oriented toward machine translation. The study of the translation process in humans is no more than a preliminary step in semiotic research.

Semiotic theory seems very optimistic. Nevertheless, it provides a new perspective on some aspects of translation and has brought to light the following points:

1.   The most distinctive trait of human translation is its *creativity*, for translation involves choices that are not determined by pre-set rules.
2.   Whatever the nature of the text to be translated, the goal is always to *transmit information without changing it*.
3.   Fidelity of translation can only be defined in *functional* terms.
4.   The information required to understand a message is provided by the *linguistic context* and the supplementary *extra-linguistic information*.
5.   *Both types of analysis (linguistic and extra-linguistic) are necessary* before one can select signs in the output code that match those of the input message.

Linguistic Theory

John C. Catford takes a strictly linguistic point of view and attempts to define and explain translation by means of the categories contained in a general theory of language. He begins from the premise: "Since translation has to do with language, the analysis and description of translation-processes must make considerable use of categories set up for the description of languages. It must, in other words, draw upon a theory of language—a general linguistic theory."[14] As an attempt at synthesis, Catford's theory is exemplary in its rigour, but it offers no new linguistic insights into translation. Catford has reformulated in his own fashion the classic definitions of translation without really making them any clearer. He defines free translation, for example, as follows: "A *free* translation is always *unbounded*—equivalents shunt up and down the rank scale, but tend to be at the higher ranks—sometimes between larger units than the sentence."[15] The work is a series of definitions like this one, put in equally rarefied language. Catford concludes that "the SL and TL items rarely have 'the same meaning' in the linguistic sense; but they can function in the same situation. In total translation, SL and TL texts or items are translation equivalents when they are *interchangeable in a given situation*."[16] He simply re-affirms that word-for-word translation is unacceptable, because words drawn from two different languages will not have

---

14.   Catford, *A Linguistic Theory of Translation*, p. vii.
15.   Ibid., p. 25 (Catford's italics).
16.   Ibid., p. 49 (Catford's italics). SL = Source Language; TL = Target Language.

the same signification within their respective codes and, therefore, translation equivalents must be based on equivalence of situation, not on correspondence between words.

What is original about *A Linguistic Theory of Translation* is its description of four very specialized types of translation: phonological, graphological, grammatical, and lexical. Catford calls them forms of restricted translation and says: "by *restricted translation* we mean: *replacement of SL textual material by equivalent TL textual material, at only one level,* that is, translation performed only at the phonological, or at the graphological level, or at only one of the two levels of grammar and lexis."[17] This type of fragmentary translation—or more properly, transcoding (see p. 42)—occurs infrequently, if at all, in the daily work of a professional translator. It is a rare exception, and it has very little to do with translation defined as an operation on the overall meaning of messages. It is of little consequence in the analysis of the cognitive processes of translation.

Overall, then, Catford's linguistic theory is of no more use to the translator struggling to render a text in another language than Ljudskanov's semiotic theory. Nor can its categories and definitions be used as a framework for organizing a program of instruction based on practical exercises. As we will see, one of the reasons why the theory has no pedagogical applications is that the author, like many linguists who study translation, attempts to explain the dynamics of discourse only in terms of the categories used to describe language. In discourse analysis—the linguistics of texts—the categories of general or descriptive linguistics are not sufficient, because the objects of study are not the same.

Sociolinguistic Theory

Eugene A. Nida, one of the most influential theorists in the field of translation, took up the essence of his earlier work, *Toward a Science of Translating* (1964), in *The Theory and Practice of Translation*, written with Charles Taber (1969), which he offers as a sort of "translation manual." He says in the preface: "This second volume presents certain of these same theories in a pedagogically oriented order, designed to assist the translator to master the theoretical elements as well as to gain certain practical skills in learning how to carry out the procedures."[18] This attempt to link theory and practice represents an innovation in the methodology of translation teaching whose significance has not been sufficiently appreciated. The book includes more than forty "problems," or practical exercises directly linked to theoretical

---

17. Ibid., p. 22 (Catford's italics).
18. Nida and Taber, *The Theory and Practice of Translation*, p. vii.

points. These practical exercises are almost all based on examples drawn from the Bible, an approach that Nida justifies by saying that it "reflects both the immediate concerns of *those for whom the book has been specifically prepared* and the background experience of the authors."[19] "The Theory and Practice of *Bible* Translation" would be a more accurate title for the book, because that is what it primarily deals with (although several observations could be applied to other types of translation).

As a translation manual, the work is, nonetheless, a model in its field, because its authors link principles and practice, which few theorists have bothered to do. Unfortunately, because it focuses on the problems peculiar to a very specific type of text—the Scriptures—this method cannot be directly applied to practical training in other types of translation. What Nida and Taber so admirably did for Bible translation has to be done for literary, technical, and advertising translation. Translation could then be taught more systematically. Nida and Taber, to their great credit, have shown the way.

It did not take long for Nida to realize the limitations of a purely linguistic approach to translation: "Because translating always involves communication within the context of interpersonal relations, the model for such activity must be a communication model, and the principles must be primarily sociolinguistic in the broad sense of the term. As such, translating becomes a part of the even broader field of anthropological semiotics."[20] Given the nature of Biblical texts, and the great diversity of languages into which they must be translated and civilizations for which they must be adapted, it is not surprising that Nida emphasized culture. He also made a valuable contribution by showing that in order to translate one must not only know a language, but also be familiar with the customs, mores, and civilization of those who speak it. His theory therefore extends far beyond the boundaries of general linguistics within which Catford chose to stay. Acknowledging that translation cannot be fully explained by a purely linguistic model, and wishing to link his sociolinguistic theory to communication theory, Nida abandoned the terms "target" and "target language" in favour of "receptor" and "receptor language." This terminology is evidence of his desire to adapt the divine word to the consciousness of each people, choosing new symbolism where necessary, but without losing any of the original meaning or sacred character of the message. Given Nida's outlook, it is easy to understand why, in his view, "only a sociolinguistic approach to translation is ultimately valid."[21]

---

19. Ibid., (my italics). Nida has had over twenty-five years' experience in Bible translation and is head of the translation department of the American Bible Society.
20. Nida, "A Framework for the Analysis and Evaluation of Theories of Translation," p. 78.
21. Ibid., p. 77.

However, the anthropological aspects of Nida's theory should not cause us to lose sight of its linguistic background. Indeed, many chapters in the two books are of greater interest to linguists than to translators. The works are more remarkable for their excellent synthesis of the advances made by modern linguists in the field of translation than for the originality of their ideas. For example, the analysis of the grammatical relationship between the words of certain verses of the Scriptures (by the method described on p. 51ff of *The Theory and Practice of Translation*) is a straightforward application of the deep structures of transformational grammar. This method of analysis, by which a statement is broken down into a series of basic structures called "kernels," might do for Bible translation, but it would be unworkable and inappropriate for pragmatic texts. Furthermore, its value is questionable from a methodological point of view. The author himself admits that "such back-transformations are not to be used as a model for translation."[22] This example shows how Nida the linguist uses the categories of descriptive linguistics to facilitate the teaching of Bible translation. The danger lies in generalizing this method to all types of text.

Principles and Pedagogy

The teacher seeking a way out of the empirical rut will look for a theory that proposes a series of steps specific to translation in order to organize his teaching systematically. The ideal theory of translation, from his point of view, would not be confined to abstract speculation, but would describe translation in terms that were neither too general nor too specific. Rules that are too specific would be too limited in their scope and would ultimately amount to a sort of "Fowler's" of translation, while laws that are too general would be of no practical value. From a pedagogical point of view, a theory's worth is determined largely by the extent to which it reflects the realities of language and can be applied to them.

Although they include a rich and coherent set of relevant observations regarding translation as a general phenomenon, the theories of Ljudskanov, Catford, and Nida are of little help to the instructor who wishes to be more systematic in teaching how to translate pragmatic texts, either because they are too abstract (Ljudskanov and Catford) or because they are too closely associated with a specific type of translation (Nida). Setting a goal is one thing; finding concrete means of reaching it is another matter altogether. Any theoretical enquiry tends inevitably toward abstraction and generalization; but the theorist, rather than hovering at that level as Ljudskanov and

---

22. Nida and Taber, *The Theory and Practice of Translation*, p. 47.

Catford do, should attempt to come back down to the concrete realities of language. Only then will the gap between the theory and practice of translation be bridged, as it must be. Although their value is undeniable, the three theories mentioned generally have little to do with the everyday concerns of professional translators, and so cannot meet pedagogical requirements. They are better suited to informing translators than forming them, and are of little assistance in teaching students to translate pragmatic texts.

Stylistique comparée du français et de l'anglais, on the other hand, is both a "theory" and a "practical treatise" on translation; it is subtitled "A Method of Translation."[23] Unlike the other theories, this major contribution by Jean-Paul Vinay and Jean Darbelnet focuses on techniques for English-French and French-English translation. Indeed, one of the authors' stated intentions is to provide general translators with advice and practical guidelines for exercising their craft.

Is comparative stylistics, then, the ideal instrument for training translators? Is the art of translation based on the comparison of equivalents? Does this method help develop the ability to manipulate language so as to communicate meaning in a given situation, thus meeting the specific goal of the translation teacher (as stated on p. 27)? If the intellectual process involved in translation is one of comparison, practical training of future translators can take the form of exercises in finding and comparing equivalents; translation and its theoretical explanation would then be completely discontinuous. If, on the other hand, the comparative model does not match the translator's thought process, the teaching methodology will have to rest upon some other theoretical foundation.

Comparative stylistics, therefore, raises four basic epistemological questions:
1.   Is the translator's approach a comparative one?
2.   Does the comparative model account for the genesis of the translation process?
3.   Can the analysis and classification of translation equivalences take the place of a theory of translation?
4.   Is comparative stylistics really a method of translation?

In order to make our critical study of *Stylistique comparée du français et de l'anglais* easier, and to answer these four questions, we must first distinguish between transcoding and true translation. The first operation produces "transcoded" equivalents, the second, "contextual" equivalents.

---

23.   "LA STYLITRAD [théorie de la stylistique comparée] ou la vraie théorie de la traduction." Vinay, "Regards sur l'évolution des théories," p. 13.

TRANSLATION AND TRANSCODING

The statements contained in a message are made up of linguistic signs, the sign being a "two-sided psychological entity"[24] that brings together a signified, or concept, and a signifier, which is the sensory (oral or written) counterpart of the signified.

These signs can be analyzed on two levels: that of the language system, and that of language use. In other words, they can be analyzed in terms of their signification, or in terms of their meaning. The *signification* of a word is that to which the word refers in the abstract system of language. Any given word can have more than one signification, which can be apprehended out of context; that is, independently of any discourse situation. This makes it possible to compile significations in lexicographical works.

Words also have a value, which is a product of the close interdependence of lexical units in a language system. (See p. 91, note 9). Value is, in fact, just one element of the signification. Saussure proposed a now-classic example to illustrate this subtle concept:

> Modern French *mouton* can have the same signification as English *sheep* but not the same value, and this for several reasons, particularly because in speaking of a piece of meat ready to be served on the table, English uses *mutton* instead of *sheep*. The difference in value between *sheep* and *mouton* is due to the fact that *sheep* has beside it a second term while the French word does not.[25]

Value is thus a purely structural notion. The speakers of a language are not immediately aware of it; on the contrary, the linguist must make a particular effort to discover it. The translator, for his part, operates at the level of meaning and not of value. While the linguist analyzes language, the translator analyzes discourse.

A word has a meaning when it is contained in a concrete statement, in a linguistic sequence generated by an individual speech event. The meaning of words and syntagmas is the relevant signification that remains after the context or situation has eliminated all other significations. The meaning of a message arises from the combination and interdependence of the relevant significations of the message's words and syntagmas, enriched by non-linguistic factors. It is an expression of the author's intention.

Thus, every word has one or several significations, and every utterance is a series of words invested with meaning. However, in order to have communicative value, that is, in order to have a *single* meaning, an utterance

---

24. Saussure, *Course in General Linguistics*, p. 66 [p. 99 in original French edition]. All quotations are from this edition, translated by W. Baskin.
25. Ibid., pp. 115-116 [p. 160].

must be actualized in a speech event and refer to either a concrete or an abstract entity. Signification is *given* by language, while meaning must be *built* from linguistic significations combined with non-linguistic factors. Signification is to language as a system what meaning is to discourse, and the study of sentences in isolation is to linguistics what the study of utterances in context is to modern rhetoric.

As we will see in greater detail later, understanding an utterance and understanding the meaning of an isolated sentence are two entirely different things. That is why "the study of discourse—rhetoric—cannot be regarded simply as a development in the study of language—linguistics."[26] Nor can the analysis of a dynamic cognitive process like translation be regarded as a simple application of the study of linguistics. The linguist is concerned with sentences, the rhetorician with utterances. The translator must understand the successive utterances in a text. But what is it to understand an utterance?

> It is (among other things) to recognize a sentence of the language, to retain one and only one of the possible meanings of that sentence, to ascribe a value to referential expressions, to detect what is left unstated. These intellectual operations are based on grammatical knowledge, but also on an understanding of the world; they are a kind of performance; they are rhetorical rather than linguistic. We all continually perform such rhetorical operations without really being conscious of doing so. The result of those operations—the conceptual interpretation of the utterance—is so obvious to us that it takes a serious effort to grasp the complexity of the work we have unconsciously done. We are generally content to admit that the situation, the context, determine how the utterance is interpreted. But we are still very far from understanding the mechanism by which this occurs.[27]

In this sense, rhetoric could, by and large, be defined as "the way in which utterances bring into play and modify the shared knowledge"[28] of two interlocutors or of a writer and a reader.

---

26. "L'étude du discours—la rhétorique—ne saurait être un simple développement de l'étude de la langue—la linguistique." Sperber, "Rudiments de rhétorique cognitive," p. 389.

27. "C'est (entre autres choses), y reconnaître une phrase de la langue, retenir un, et un seul des sens de cette phrase, donner une valeur aux expressions référentielles, calculer les sous-entendus. Ces opérations intellectuelles s'appuient sur la compétence grammaticale, mais aussi sur la connaissance du monde; elles relèvent de la performance; elles sont rhétoriques et non point linguistiques. De telles opérations rhétoriques, nous en accomplissons tous à chaque instant de notre vie sans trop nous en rendre compte. Le résultat de ces opérations, c'est-à-dire l'interprétation conceptuelle de l'énoncé, s'impose à nous avec une telle évidence qu'il faut un sérieux effort pour mesurer la complexité du travail inconsciemment accompli. On se contente généralement d'admettre que la situation, le contexte, détermine l'interprétation de l'énoncé. Mais le mécanisme de cette détermination n'a jamais été décrit, il s'en faut de beaucoup." Ibid., p. 392.

28. ". . . la manière dont les énoncés mettent en jeu et modifient le savoir partagé." Ibid., p. 392.

Rhetoric, defined as the study of discourse, provides the theoretical framework for the method of instruction proposed here. Discourse is made up of thoughts expressed symbolically and communicated. In searching for an equivalent, the translator analyzes discourse. Unlike most linguists, who analyze words and sentences in and for themselves, the translator analyzes the text at a higher level, looking beyond the individual word, sentence, or isolated utterance. According to the *Dictionnaire de didactique des langues*:

> The speech event as such constitutes the discourse situation in which a linguistic manifestation called an utterance is actualized. Speech event and utterance are related to each other as cause and effect; indeed, the utterance can be extracted from the circumstances of its production (the discourse situation) and analyzed separately, from a purely linguistic point of view. In analyzing the speech event, on the other hand, one must take into account the interlocutors (their intentions, their relationship to one another) and the referent. For this reason, linguists have often regarded the speech event as falling outside the scope of their analysis.[29]

One of the major weaknesses of (linguistic) theories of translation is that they have not ventured far enough beyond the word and sentence. As James S. Holmes so rightly pointed out:

> One of the great drawbacks of practically all the linguistic translation theories that we have had up to now has been that they have had to work with a linguistics which is only interested in the sentence and linguistic phenomena below the sentence level; linguistics itself in the structural period and even in the transformational period had been very frightened of going beyond the sentence. Translation, on the other hand, . . . is so obviously a question not of translating a series of sentences but of translating a text.[30]

We will return later to the distinction between sentence-by-sentence translation and contextual translation, and to its pedagogical consequences.

The theoretical approach adopted here necessitates a redefinition of the concept of translation—the term has so many different meanings that it could lead to confusion. "Translation" (the result) can be distinguished from "translating activity" (a series of intellectual operations) in the same way that Piaget distinguishes "perception" from "perceptual activity." In

---

29. "L'énonciation en tant que telle constitue la situation du discours, qui actualise la manifestation linguistique qu'est l'énoncé. On peut opposer énoncé à énonciation comme on oppose le résultat à la cause, et même extraire l'énoncé des circonstances de sa production (situation de discours) pour l'analyser isolément, d'un point de vue purement linguistique. L'énonciation, elle, implique la prise en considération des interlocuteurs (intentions, types de rapports) et du référent. À ce titre, les linguistes ont souvent considéré qu'elle ne relevait pas de leur domaine d'analyse." Galisson and Coste, *Dictionnaire*, at entry for "énonciation."
30. Holmes, "Translation Theory," p. 57.

Piaget's terminology, perception is a *"resultant,* or stabilized totality,"* while "perceptual activity" refers to *"efforts* to explore a figure, or to explore the relationship between figures." He adds that "perceptual activity like this has a great deal in common with intelligence. Similar mechanisms come into play."[31] Telling time from a clock, for example, involves a whole series of more or less conscious operations by which one locates the clock on the wall, studies the position of the hands on the dial, recognizes the numbers they are pointing to, and so on. This analysis of figures corresponds to the "perceptual activity," which results in "perception." In the same way, what we refer to as the translating activity represents the intellectual effort needed to create a conceptual equivalence. From a psychological point of view, this activity consists in untangling the complex web of logical relations that bind a text together.

This distinction is of the utmost importance in the pedagogy of translation, where the point is not to compare performances (that is, to compare texts that have already been translated), but to give students a grasp of the process of semantic transfer. The synonymous expressions "translating activity," "translating operation," "translation process," "translation mechanism," and "act of translating" seem preferable to the less explicit "translation" for describing the psycholinguistic operations, defined by complex algorithms, that take place in the translator's brain.

From a methodological point of view, translation theory and pedagogy must clearly distinguish between two broad categories of equivalences produced in the passage from one language to another. In everyday usage, word or sentence equivalences are called "translations," as are message equivalences, that is, equivalences of utterances in context or in situation. In Saussurean terms, the first type of equivalence is established at the level of language as a system, whereas the second type arises out of the use of language in a given situation. There would be no need to draw this distinction if word and message equivalences were both established by the same process and their success in rendering the meaning of the original evaluated by the same criteria. This is certainly not so. In the case of equivalence between isolated words, the goal is to match two signifiers to a single signified; in the case of equivalence between messages, the translator's aim is to faithfully reproduce the thoughts communicated by the author.

In translating, for example, it is not enough to state that "sympathetic" in English should be rendered by "compréhensif" in French, and not by its formal twin "sympathique." By doing that, one simply contrasts two signifiers that might be linked to the same concept by a faulty knowledge of the two languages when, in fact, despite their similar form, they refer to

---

31.　Evans, *Jean Piaget*, p. 10 (my italics).

quite different concepts. What is more, the statement must be accompanied by lengthy explanations. Some senses of "sympathetic" are indeed rendered by "sympathique." In medical terminology, the accepted French equivalent of "sympathetic nervous system" is "système nerveux sympathique." Of even greater importance to the translator is the fact that, although "sympathetic" can mean "compréhensif," it is not always correctly rendered by that term in French, *even when it is being used in that particular sense.*

For example, let us consider the following excerpt from a letter by a senior civil servant politely rejecting a social worker's suggestion: "While I am more than sympathetic to the recommendations of the social worker, we have to remember that . . . ." It would be unidiomatic, and indeed nonsensical, to write, in French, "Bien que je sois très compréhensif envers la recommandation . . . ." Equivalents such as "Bien que je sois particulièrement *réceptif* à la recommandation du travailleur social . . ." or "Bien que je *juge* la recommandation du travailleur social *tout à fait valable . . .*" would, on the other hand, be quite appropriate.

This brief example provides a vivid illustration of the difference between transcoding (an exercise in contrasting the potentialities of two linguistic codes) and translation in the proper sense of the word (an exercise in interpreting meaning). The techniques used in language analysis are not the same as those used in discourse analysis. Bronislav Malinowski says that translation "is never a matter of substituting one word for another, but always of translating the situation as a whole."[32] He adds that "if translation is thought of as the act of drawing an equal sign between 'un' and *one*, it can never be more than a rough, makeshift solution that must be supplemented by a long series of explanations"[33] (which could just as easily have been said of the example I gave using "sympathetic" and "compréhensif"). This explains why bilingual dictionaries do not qualify as translated works.

Language equivalence is established with reference to language as a system of relationships and oppositions. Discourse equivalence is established with reference to a communicative situation through a linguistic context. This is why it is more difficult to judge the accuracy of a translated text than the correspondence between isolated words from different languages, such as "sympathetic" and "compréhensif." Language equivalence involves only the comparison of potentials, because linguistic signs are, by nature, indeter-

---

32.   ". . . ne consiste jamais à substituer un mot à un autre, mais toujours à traduire globalement des situations." Malinowski, "Théorie ethnographique du langage," p. 246.
33.   "Si l'on conçoit la traduction comme l'acte qui consiste à tracer un signe égale entre 'un' et *one* ce ne peut être qu'un expédient provisoire et approximatif que l'on doit compléter par une longue série de données." Ibid., p. 248. Other contexts in which "sympathetic" means "compréhensif" are: The workers went on a sympathetic strike/Les travailleurs ont fait une grève de solidarité; Before departing, she said a few sympathetic words/Avant de partir, elle lui a adressé quelques mots d'encouragement.

minate. In the interest of precise terminology, "transcoded" should therefore apply only to equivalences established without reference to any real
communication situation, and "translated" should be used exclusively of
contextual equivalences.

Meaning of Lexical Units

Better than any analysis of a single language, translation demonstrates the
fact that in discourse a word can have a completely different meaning from
the one normally associated with that word taken in isolation. In the following
description of a submarine called the EEL, the word "smooth" means
"hydrodynamique" (hydrodynamic), a definition that would not be found
in any bilingual dictionary:

> The EEL's surface is perfectly *smooth* with the forward diving planes, rear
> rudder, radio and sonar bubbles as the only protrusions.

Translation:

> On a donné au EEL une forme parfaitement *hydrodynamique*; seuls les ailerons
> avant de plongée, le gouvernail et les dômes logeant la radio et le sonar font
> saillie.

In this sentence the word "smooth" acquires its meaning from its association with the words that surround and influence it. The context effectively
eliminates the potential significations so that the one signification relevant
in this particular context remains, and polysemy vanishes immediately. This
confirms that semantic transfer between languages can take place on two
levels, that of the potential significations of linguistic signs ("smooth" =
"lisse," "égal," "uni"; in other words, all the significations found in
dictionaries) or that of the meaning of the message ("smooth" = "hydrodynamique" in a given context).

Unilingual dictionaries record the most common meanings that words
have acquired through repeated use. They are lexicographical museums, in
that they preserve the numerous fixed, institutionalized significations of the
words that make up the linguistic heritage of a society. However, dictionaries give only a slight indication of the countless meanings that words can
have in actual use. Lexicographers, those "harmless drudges" (as Samuel
Johnson defined them), are interested chiefly in fixed relationships between
signified and signifier. (The same could be said of semanticists.) In their
dictionary entries they attempt to define words, but the definitions are never
complete. It is unrealistic to try to collect all the meanings that a word can
have in a speech event. By recording all the stable or fixed meanings of words,

compilers of dictionaries provide the users of a language with an extremely useful decoding tool, but one whose limitations must be recognized.

Everything I have said about unilingual dictionaries applies equally to general bilingual dictionaries, which are sometimes improperly called "translation dictionaries." They are useful works, providing equivalents for the most common significations of the words in each language, but they certainly do not explore all the semantic possibilities of words used in context. Teachers cannot make this point too often to student translators who seem to naïvely believe that a bilingual dictionary has the answer to all questions. To defend a solution rejected by the teacher they simply argue that "It's in the dictionary," as if that were the sole justification necessary. For the word "smooth," *Harrap's Standard French and English Dictionary* gives these common meanings: lisse, uni, égal, sans asperités, poli; glacé (paper); sans rides (forehead); douce, satinée (skin); calme, unie, plate (sea); doux; sans heurts; régulier (operation); silencieux (movement); moelleux (wine); coulant (style); égale, facile (mood); doucereux; mielleux; and a few other less common equivalents such as glabre (chin) and paterne (tone).

The translator who searches no further than the most commonly used signification of a word or the one that comes to mind automatically ("smooth" = "lisse") risks attributing an incorrect meaning to a word. That explains the lapses typical of novice or incompetent translators who proceed by looking up every other word in the dictionary. As Tatiana Slama-Cazacu says, "Signs are not understood in isolation, despite what the clumsy translator thinks who looks up each word in a dictionary, writes down its most common translation, and then joins them all together in the naïve belief that by adding up the translations he will somehow arrive at the meaning of the sentence."[34] The meaning of a word, sentence, or whole text is grasped by means of interpretation. *Translation is an exercise in interpretation, an intelligent analysis of the text.*

Meaning of Utterances

Everything said in the previous section about words is true of sentences. In a text, a sentence can have a meaning other than that of the sum of its decoded linguistic signs. "Words taken in isolation have only potential signification; sentences out of context have only potential meaning," says Marianne

---

34. "Les signes ne sont pas compris isolément, comme pourrait le croire un traducteur maladroit qui noterait, pour chaque mot, la traduction trouvée dans le dictionnaire et qui les unirait par la suite en faisant le total de leurs formes typiques, avec la naïve conviction qu'il pourrait surprendre le sens de la phrase par ce procédé additif." Slama-Cazacu, *Langage et contexte*, p. 227.

Lederer.[35]

An example is the sentence: "Her surgeon was able to do just that," taken from a popular article on medicine in *Time* (April 1975). If the signs making up this sentence are decoded out of context, at least two different meanings are possible:

1.   That is exactly what her surgeon was able to do (c'est tout à fait ce que son chirurgien pouvait faire),

2.   That is all that her surgeon was able to do (c'est tout ce que son chirurgien pouvait faire).

Without a context it is impossible to interpret the original sentence with absolute certainty. Moreover, the identity of the person represented by the possessive "her" is not known, nor is the reason why she consulted a surgeon. "That" gives no information on what the surgeon could or could not do. Each version is grammatically correct, but gives rise to a host of different meanings.

However, as soon as the sentence is put back into its context, all the ambiguities are cleared up, and only one meaning is possible. "Her" refers to a fifty-four-year-old New York woman, Joan Dawson, who underwent breast surgery in 1970, and "that" refers to her desire to put a prosthesis in place of the missing breast. The analysis of the statement in context is no longer a strictly linguistic operation, but one that belongs to discourse analysis. The sentence is part of the following paragraph:

Rebuilding the Breast

After the removal of her left breast because of cancer in 1970, Mrs. Joan Dawson, 54, of New York City, spent the next three years battling depression and a sense of loss. Then she decided to do something about it. Most women in the same situation turn to a psychiatrist. Mrs. Dawson (not her real name) went to her doctor and asked him to rebuild her missing breast. "I didn't want to be made into a sensational beauty," she explained. "I just wanted to be restored." Her surgeon was able to do just that. In two separate operations, he implanted a silicone-filled sac under the skin where the breast had been removed, then reduced the size of the other breast to make it more nearly resemble the new one. The result is not a duplication of Mrs. Dawson's pre-1970 figure, but she is delighted nevertheless. Says she: "I can finally look at myself in the mirror without wincing."[36]

The context determines the signification of each sign (by nature indeterminate), and thus supports *one* meaning. Temporarily unambiguous, the

---

35.   "Les mots pris isolément n'ont que des virtualités de signification, les phrases séparées de leur contexte n'ont que des virtualités de sens." Lederer, "La traduction: transcoder ou réexprimer?", p. 8.

36.   The complete article is reproduced in Appendix 1.

sentences are linked together in a network of linguistic and non-linguistic relationships, and polysemy is not a problem.[37] The context ensures that the potential ambiguity pointed out earlier does not occur; it does not even enter the reader's mind. The relationships among sentences in a text are analogous (but not identical) to those among the words in a language: *just as the interdependence among words gives each word its conceptual value in the semiotic system of language,[38] the* interdependence of utterances *in a message gives each utterance its single, unambiguous meaning.* Of course, in language, values are relatively stable, while in a text, the statements form a complementary relationship only for the duration of a message. That is why no two texts are identical.

Once translation is viewed as an operation that consists of reformulating a meaning and not simply reproducing a syntactic arrangement of words having many potential significations, the context has the effect of multiplying ten-fold the linguistic means the translator has at his disposal for re-expressing the meaning of the original message in the target language.[39] That is one of the postulates of discourse analysis. The translator has creative freedom, in Alexander Ljudskanov's sense,[40] and this distinguishes him from the transcoder. The linguistic and cognitive context of the statement "Her surgeon was able to do just that" compels the translator to adopt the first solution, "C'est tout à fait ce que son chirurgien pouvait faire," rather than the second one. But, given this context, he could also use the idiomatic expression "Elle avait frappé à la bonne porte" (literally: "She had knocked at the right door"). Students in a translation workshop translated the text as follows:

La reconstitution des seins

Une Newyorkaise de 54 ans, Mme Joan Dawson* subit en 1970 l'ablation du sein gauche atteint de cancer et passa les trois années suivantes à lutter contre la dépression et le traumatisme de la mutilation. Un beau jour, elle décide d'agir. La plupart des femmes, en pareil cas, vont s'en remettre à un psychiatre, mais Mme Dawson, elle, retourne chez son médecin pour qu'il lui refasse son sein. "Je ne voulais pas qu'il me transforme en une beauté sensationnelle, a-t-elle

---

37.   Sometimes ambiguity is deliberately introduced into a message. Then it is "equivocal," according to the distinction made by H. Bénac in his *Dictionnaire des synonymes*. If the equivocation is involuntary it can be considered a failure of communication.
38.   "The conceptual side of value is made up solely of relations and differences with respect to the other terms of language." Saussure, *Course in General Linguistics*, 117 [p. 163].
39.   La Bruyère believed that of all the different ways of expressing a single thought only one was right. ("Entre toutes les différentes expressions qui peuvent rendre une seule de nos pensées, il n'y en a qu'une qui soit la bonne.") *Les caractères* (Paris: Gallimard, 1965) p. 25. Textual analysis invalidates this view.
40.   According to Ljudskanov, any process that calls for one or more choices not governed by previously established rules is creative. (*Traduction humaine*, vol. 2, p. 53.)

expliqué par la suite, mais simplement qu'il élimine les traces de l'amputation."
Elle avait frappé à la bonne porte. Le chirurgien inséra sous la peau un sac
de silicone en remplacement de la glande mammaire et, par une seconde intervention, il réduisit les proportions de l'autre sein pour le rendre à peu près
de la même grosseur que le sein artificiel. Mme Dawson n'a pas retrouvé sa
silhouette d'avant 1970, mais elle est enchantée du résultat. "Je peux enfin
me regarder dans un miroir sans grimacer," a-t-elle confié.
*Ce nom est fictif.

Just as it was impossible to predict, without knowing the context, that
the word "smooth" could mean "hydrodynamique," so it would be impossible to guess, through a strictly lexical and grammatical analysis, that the
English statement "Her surgeon was able to do just that," could correspond
to the French "Elle avait frappé à la bonne porte." In essence, "The language
system assigns words a certain signification, but language use enriches them
with notions that from a purely lexicological point of view would be
unimaginable."[41]

The contextual equivalent "Elle avait frappé à la bonne porte" raises
several points. First, this translation is exemplary not because of its form,
but because of the principle underlying it. This example of a reformulation
that is notably different from the linguistic signs of the original was chosen
to better illustrate this principle, which is of paramount importance in both
the theory and teaching of translation. Second, this solution is solid proof
that translation is as closely related to rhetoric as it is to linguistics, and that
the translator analyzes discourse, not just words or sentences. Third, the
contextual equivalent "Elle avait frappé à la bonne porte" is only one possible
translation. Other solutions could be found, such as: "C'est tout à fait ce
que son chirurgien pouvait faire" (which has already been mentioned), "Son
chirurgien a pu exaucer son désir," or "C'est exactement ce qu'a fait son
chirurgien." Finally, it would be a mistake to assume that the formulation
most unlike the original is the best one.[42] *The accuracy of an equivalence
is measured by how closely the concepts match, not by the similarity or
dissimilarity of the forms in which the concepts are expressed.* Whether it
sticks closely to the original or not, a translation will be awkward if the target

41. "La langue attribue une signification aux mots, mais la parole les enrichit de notions
inimaginables au seul plan lexicologique." Lederer, "La traduction: transcoder ou réexprimer?"
p. 9.
42. Georges Mounin has coined the term "hypertranslation" to describe certain translators'
obsessive use of expressions whose form is as far removed as possible from that of the original,
even where there is an expression available that matches the source language expression word
for word. *(Les belles infidèles,* p. 84.) "Translationitis," at the other extreme, is the irrational
fear of never communicating the full expressive power of foreign words. (Ibid., p. 34.) This
second fault has also been called "overtranslation."

language concepts are not well matched to the concepts of the source language.

Other examples drawn from the same text illustrate how the context can make a freer translation possible: "le traumatisme de la mutilation" for "a sense of loss" (this syntagma will be analyzed in greater detail in the next chapter); "un beau jour" for "then"; "qu'il élimine les traces de l'amputation" for "to be restored"; "glande mammaire" for "breast"; and "le sein artificiel" for "the new one." Each text is a concrete, individual instance of language use; bilingual discourse analysis confirms this.

In conclusion, to study translation from a strictly linguistic point of view is to handicap oneself by merely transposing the significations of words without ever grasping their meaning. As Pergnier has said: "The linguistics of language is for the most part an 'antisemantics' that detracts from the study of the *meaning* of messages."[43] In other words, transcoding is not translating, for the overall meaning of an utterance cannot be communicated merely by transposing verbal significations.

Translation can therefore be defined as the operation by which the relevant signification of linguistic signs is determined through reference to a meaning as formulated in a message, which is then fully reconstructed in the signs of another language. Equivalences established on a word-for-word or sentence-for-sentence basis are the product of a strictly linguistic analysis (a transcoding operation); those that arise from the dynamics of a discourse are the product of interpretation (a translating operation). As we shall see later in this chapter, interpretive analysis is a basic step in the translation process; without it, there can be no translation.

It sometimes happens that the translation of an utterance is the same as its simple transcoding; the translation is then called "literal." This similarity of form, however, is coincidental and has nothing to do with the reformulation of meaning. This purely fortuitous occurrence does not obviate the interpretive analysis that must always precede re-expression.

One other point should be mentioned. Certain brief utterances, on road signs or billboards, for example, are not embedded in a context but relate directly to a situation. These utterances may be said to constitute messages in themselves. Vinay and Darbelnet's *Stylistique comparée* begins with examples of this type: "SLOW MEN AT WORK," "DÉFENSE DE DOUBLER," "SLIPPERY WHEN WET," "RALENTIR," "PRIORITÉ À DROITE." One should not conclude, however, that the absence of a context eliminates the need for interpretive analysis in translating these road signs or any analogous utterance. Even if the context is skeletal or altogether

---

43.   "La linguistique de la langue est en grande partie un 'anti-sémantique', et va à l'encontre de l'étude du *sens* des messages particuliers." Pergnier, "L'envers des mots," p. 97 (Pergnier's italics).

nonexistent, it is absolutely essential that the utterance be considered in relation to the communication situation in which it occurs. Utterances are usually situated within a context. The erroneous belief that context can be ignored in postulating translation equivalents may have arisen in part because of these utterances that in themselves constitute messages.

Drawing the distinction between translation in the strict sense and inter-linguistic transcoding was a prerequisite to dissecting the intellectual process involved in translation. Now, by analyzing how a translation is created, I will determine whether the process is comparative or not. I will also identify the characteristics specific to the activity of translating, which will form the basis of the curriculum. This detailed analysis of the cognitive process of translation will enable me to determine, through a critique of *Stylistique comparée*, whether the categories proposed in that "method of translation" are actually of use in the re-expression of the ideas contained in a text.

ANALYSIS OF THE TRANSLATION PROCESS

The basis for my analysis of the intellectual mechanisms involved in trans-lating will be the title of a *Time* magazine article about the unprecedented cold wave that struck the Northern United States in early 1977.[44] The title is "The Icy Grip Tightens." Broadly speaking, there are three stages in the development of a translation equivalence: comprehension, reformulation, and verification. Each stage can be divided into subsidiary operations: comprehension is based on decoding linguistic signs and grasping meaning, reformulation is a matter of reasoning by analogy and re-wording concepts, and verification involves back-interpreting and choosing a solution. We shall now attempt to get inside the translator's brain in order to follow him through the complex cognitive process of translation.

Comprehension

In the first stage of the process, comprehending the text, the translator essen-tially attempts to determine what the author wanted to say. Obviously, one cannot grasp the meaning of a text simply by reading it. It is quite possible to visualize the graphic signs of a text written in a foreign language or to mentally pronounce the sounds they symbolize without understanding the meaning of the signs. This purely physical act of perception must be accom-panied by a mental activity that may be called interpretive analysis.[45]

The written text is the physical basis of an intricately woven network of relationships that must be analyzed. These relationships fall into two broad

---

44. *Time*, Feb. 14, 1977. The opening paragraphs of the article are reproduced in Appendix 2.
45. See "Meaning of Lexical Units," chapter 2, and "Performing Interpretive Analysis," chapter 3.

categories: semantic relationships between the words and utterances of the text, and referential relationships between the utterances and non-linguistic phenomena. The network into which the signs are integrated derives its coherence from the will of the author to communicate information to the reader. The translator perusing a text to be translated thus finds himself in the same position as a unilingual reader acquainting himself with its contents. Like the reader, the translator is an active participant in the communication process. In order to discover how this silent communication by means of the written word occurs, we must determine how the reader goes about analyzing the relationships that underlie a message so as to grasp its meaning. Interpretation is crucial to comprehension for, as André Martinet has pointed out, "in communicating with language, we signal something that is not manifest by means of something that is."[46] Interpretation is thus a hermeneutic dialogue between the translator and the original text.

Comprehension takes place on two different levels: the level at which signifieds are grasped, and the level at which meaning is grasped.[47] Every word in an utterance refers both to the language system from which it draws its signification, and to the set of non-linguistic parameters that give it meaning. For the sake of clarity, comprehending signification and comprehending meaning will be treated as distinct and successive operations, even though they are in fact concurrent and overlapping.

Decoding Signs

Understanding signifieds, whatever their referents, is a decoding operation performed at the level of the linguistic system. The conceptual content of words is ascertained through lexical and grammatical analysis. Using his knowledge of English vocabulary, the translator calls up in his memory the signification of the individual words in the utterance "The Icy Grip Tightens." In contrast to the computer, which deals with forms, the translator is able to identify concepts mediated by linguistic signs.[48]

However, understanding involves more than the ability to recognize signifieds. It is also necessary, at this first level of comprehension, to discern the pattern of abstract relationships uniting the words of a sentence. For example, it is difficult to find any meaning in a series of words such as "paper," "wash," "concrete," "greed"; but a series such as "gardener,"

---

46. "Dans la communication linguistique, on signifie quelque chose qui n'est pas manifesté au moyen de quelque chose qui l'est." Martinet, *Éléments de linguistique générale*, p. 37.
47. Seleskovitch, "Traduire," p. 87.
48. In machine translation the task of linguistics is to construct a formal language of semantic description. The numerous difficulties attending computerized translation confirm that translation—in the fullest sense of the word and defined as an interpretive process—is an act of intelligence invoking the human faculties of reason and judgement and a substantial amount of extra-linguistic knowledge.

"water," "flower," "daily" does form a unit having some significative value, even if it is somewhat unclear due to the absence of morphological markers. In a normal sentence, the purpose of the grammatical signs is to indicate clearly the relationships established by the speaker between the words and the situation. The rules in English for combining words make it obvious, for example, how "icy," "grip," and "tighten" are to be understood, and it is thus impossible to conceive of "grip" as the verbal element in the sentence.

The translator cannot just perform the lexical and grammatical analysis and then mechanically replace each signifier in the original statement by a signifier from another language intuitively selected as an equivalent. Such transcoding might produce a formulation that was grammatically correct, if the signs were arranged according to French rules for combining, as in "la prise glaciale (se) resserre" or "l'étreinte glaciale (se) resserre," but it would not be semantically appropriate. This transcoded formulation has a purely statistical value, in the sense that the equivalence is established without reference to the context and is based solely on the high *frequency* with which, in normal communication situations, "icy" is translated by "glacial," "grip" by "prise," and "tighten" by "(se) resserrer."[49] Even more importantly, because of the arbitrary nature of the choice of words, based solely on linguistics, the translator can never be sure that the string of transcoded words accurately conveys the meaning of the original. That is why transcoding is a dead end, a blind alley down which aspiring translators should learn never to stray. *Transcoding is matching similar words, translation is communicating an equivalent message.*

The comprehension of signifieds is an operation involving only the linguistic code, and therefore, however essential it may be, it will not by itself enable the translator to understand an utterance. If he limited himself to understanding signifieds, the translator's equivalences would be based on a partial interpretation. The mechanical combining of significations can produce only a vague indication of the meaning, because the signification is "nothing more than a standard supplied by the linguistic system for the

---

49. "While sentences such as 'Il fait froid' and 'It is cold' are often given as translation equivalents, it is not on account of the correspondence between the elements that compose them (or, to use Martinet's terminology, that articulate them), but because they often perform the same function in communication. The equivalence established between the two statements has nothing but a statistical basis." ("Si des énoncés comme 'il fait froid' et 'it is cold' se rencontrent souvent comme équivalents de traduction, ce n'est pas en raison de la correspondance des éléments qui les analysent (ou, selon la terminologie d'A. Martinet, qui les articulent), mais parce qu'ils remplissent souvent la même fonction dans la communication. La relation d'équivalence établie entre nos deux énoncés n'a donc d'autre fondement que statistique.") Pergnier, "Traduction et théorie linguistique," p. 38.

analysis of meaning.''[50] Translation thus presumes an operation on signifieds before an operation on meaning.

Understanding Meaning

The second step in the analysis is to define the conceptual content of an utterance more precisely by drawing on the referential context in which the utterance is embedded. The purpose of this operation is to discover, based on the *significations* of linguistic signs in the code, what the signs *mean* as parts of a message. Translation is the re-expression, not of signs, but of concepts or ideas. This alone makes it possible to bridge the gulf between languages, despite the fact that one linguistic code cannot be transposed into another.[51]

Semantics is located at the interface between the linguistic and non-linguistic worlds. It is that "part of the language where the movement from closed linguistic structures to continually open experiential structures is most visible."[52]

The text of a message does not contain the meaning, it only points to the meaning, because the signs making up the message refer to something other than themselves. Meaning may be defined as an original synthesis made at the junction of structural and situational references;[53] *interpretation is the thinking mind's discovery of the dynamic relationships between referents and linguistic signs combined in a message.*

Interpretive analysis is necessary because languages do not have separate and distinct signs for each concrete or abstract element of human experience. If there were one sign for each thing or abstract notion, polysemy would not exist, and language would in all probability be a nomenclature rather than a structural system. Translation would then simply be a matter of substituting one univocal unit for another. (If this were the case, and the interpretation inherent in the act of translating were not necessary, what would there be for the translator to do?) Words and sentences are always open to interpretation according to the situational parameters that define the communicative situation; they take on an additional dimension. By

---

50.   ". . . n'est rien d'autre qu'un *critère d'analyse* du sens fourni par le système linguistique." Pergnier, "L'envers des mots," p. 112 (Pergnier's italics). André Martinet has said "The code [is] that with which one must confront each element of a message in order to discover the meaning." ("Le code [est] ce à quoi on confronte chaque élément d'un message pour en dégager le sens.") *Éléments de linguistique générale*, p. 25.
51.   In the opening chapters of *Les problèmes théoriques de la traduction*, Mounin proves that it is impossible to explain the phenomenon of translation if it is defined as a search for matches between the signs of two languages. In "L'envers des mots," Pergnier shows that a two-dimensional conception of the signified enables one to consider it as both translatable and non-transposable from one linguistic system to another.
52.   ". . . partie de la langue où l'on passe le plus visiblement des structures linguistiques fermées, aux structures toujours ouvertes de l'expérience." Mounin, *Les problèmes théoriques*, p. 138.
53.   Pergnier, "Traduction et théorie linguistique," p. 38.

drawing language out of itself, discourse fashions a bridge between language and reality. In consequence, it is almost impossible to imagine a working model of translation that does not include interpretive analysis of significations. Indeed, researchers are currently trying to solve the problems of machine translation by means of artificial intelligence.[54] They have realized that an intelligent appraisal, or, if one prefers, an interpretive analysis, of the context is indispensable to translation. They know they have to transform adding machines into thinking machines. A machine cannot be made to translate by supplying it with conversion tables such as those used for expressing miles in kilometres or Fahrenheit temperatures in degrees Celsius. Translation is not a simple conversion of units.

Interpretation of "The Icy Grip Tightens"

It is often difficult to discern an author's intentions. For example, the title we are analyzing ("The Icy Grip Tightens") can be interpreted in two different but equally valid ways. First, it can be understood as a literary allusion to poems in which death is symbolized by cold or the clutch of a deathly hand. Such images are found in the poem by James Shirley (1596-1666) entitled "Death the Leveller":

> The glories of our blood and state
>   Are shadows, not substantial things;
> There is no armour against fate;
>   *Death lays his icy hand on kings:*
>   Sceptre and Crown
>   Must tumble down,
> And in the dust be equal made
> With the poor crooked scythe and spade.

Byron (1798-1824) also linked cold and death in his poem entitled "Youth and Age":

---

54. On artificial intelligence and contextual comprehension by computers, see Joseph Weizenbaum, "Contextual Understanding by Computers," *Communications of the Association for Computing Machinery*, vol. 10, no. 8 (1967), pp. 474-80; Roger C. Schank, *Conceptual Information Processing* (Amsterdam/Oxford: North-Holland Publishing, 1975); B.L. Nash-Webber and R.C. Schank (eds.), *Theoretical Issues in Natural Language Processing: An Interdisciplinary Workshop in Computational Linguistics, Psychology, Linguistics, Artificial Intelligence* (New Haven: Conn.: Dept. of Computer Science, Yale University, 1975); Roger C. Schank and K.M. Colby (eds.), *Computer Models of Thought and Language* (San Francisco: W.H. Freeman, 1973). For a critical review of works by Winograd, Minsky, Schank and Wanner, and Kaplan on artificial intelligence, see B. Elan Dresher and Norbert Hornstein, "On Some Supposed Contributions of Artificial Intelligence to the Scientific Study of Language," in *Cognition*, vol. 4 (1976), pp. 321-98. Rebuttals by the authors reviewed follow the article. Also see Joseph Weizenbaum, *Computer Power and Human Reason* (San Francisco: W.H. Freeman, 1976).

> Then the mortal *coldness of the soul like death* itself comes down;
> It cannot feel for others' woes, it dare not dream its own;
> That *heavy chill has frozen* o'er the fountain of our tears,
> And though the eye may sparkle still, 'tis where the *ice* appears.

Another example is found in the work of the American poet Walt Whitman (1819-92). In "Reconciliation" he uses an image similar to that employed by Shirley:

> Word over all, beautiful as the sky,
> Beautiful that war and all its needs of carnage must in time be utterly lost,
> That *the hands of the sisters Death and Night* incessantly softly wash again,
> and ever again, this soil'd world.

"The Icy Grip Tightens" thus seems to evoke poetic images. If the title is indeed interpreted this way, the French translation should, as far as possible, allude to familiar poems in French on a similar theme or evoke a reaction similar to the one produced by the English title. The translator might consider a phrase such as "L'étreinte glaciale se resserre" or "Le froid resserre son étreinte (fatidique)." According to *Le Petit Robert*, in poetry, "glacial" and "glacer" connote a deprivation of the warmth characteristic of youth and life ("Quand l'âge nous glace"). As well, "l'étreinte d'une main" and the figurative expressions "l'étreinte de la mort," "la main du destin," and "la main de la fatalité" are clichés (all in *Le Petit Robert*) corresponding to the idea expressed by "Icy Grip."

Is there any evidence in the text to justify this interpretation? The only passage that might support it is the following:

> If there is too much winter in some sections of the country, there is, strangely enough, too little elsewhere. With far less snowfall than usual, the West is suffering from a prolonged drought. . . . In Oregon, forest fires have broken out. *"Some say the world will end in fire,"* wrote Robert Frost, *"some say in ice."* Last week Americans had their choice of disasters.

Is this sufficient grounds to be certain that the author deliberately chose the title to allude to poetic images that would be familiar, at least to educated readers? The translator must always beware of falling into the trap of overtranslation. Irène de Buisseret calls it "la mirandolite," or "fièvre de Pic de la Mirandole," a form of overtranslation caused by a pretentious display of erudition, or a tendency to see allusions where none exist.[55] It is often difficult to be sure that a text does contain a literary or cultural allusion,

---

55. Buisseret, *Deux langues, six idiomes*, pp. 108-11.

and it is even more difficult to convey it by means of an equivalent when one is certain.

The second interpretation of the title results from a completely different approach: an analysis of the general situation surrounding the message "The Icy Grip Tightens." A close examination of the contextual and referential parameters suggests a different interpretation of the title, one that leads us to think that the author wanted to convey the idea of an unusually long period of cold weather affecting the northern U.S.A. To arrive at this conclusion one has to know that when the *Time* article appeared the cold snap had lasted nearly six weeks, and that *Time* had already covered the unusual weather in two major stories: "The Big Freeze" (a cover story) and "The Great Winter Hits Again" (an allusion to the movie *The Pink Panther Strikes Again*). Once in possession of these non-linguistic facts, the reader can detect in the title a hint of exasperation at the stubborn persistence of the frigid temperatures. The article even begins with the sentence, "Never before in this century had the nation been so much at the mercy of its weather." The cold snap does not relax its grip but stubbornly persists, an interpretation confirmed by the disastrous results of the long period of intense cold. Economic losses mounted as the cold wave continued. During the nation-wide catastrophe, two million workers were laid off because of plant shutdowns caused by fuel shortages, an equal number of school children stayed home because schools could not be heated, thousands of merchants closed their doors, and Florida lost almost all of its citrus crop. The first paragraphs of the article review these facts (see Appendix 2). The hardships and financial losses were caused more by the unusual duration of the cold spell than by its intensity, although daily temperatures did fall far below normal.[56]

It is immaterial which of the two interpretations is chosen; the principle involved is the same, and that is what concerns us here. Interpreting linguistic signs according to the situation and context in order to discern the author's intent, without imputing intentions to him, is a thought process that requires the translator to isolate the separate ideas contained in an utterance. For the first interpretation, the translator drew mainly upon his *cognitive inventory*, that is, the knowledge he shares with the writer of the article. For the second, the meaning of the title was made clear by the *cognitive context*, that is, the text's message and the circumstances prevailing at the time of its publication. The cognitive complements (see Figure 3) that the translator or any other speaker/reader adds to the linguistic complement prove that the meaning of an utterance or a message is much greater than the sum of the significations of the words in that utterance or message. *Language use cannot be reduced to a simple mobilization of linguistic signs.* Speakers do not express ideas

---

56. Students in a translation course interpreted the title this second way, as did a number of people who were questioned about the meaning of the title shortly after the article appeared.

by using words and sentences like a telegraph operator uses symbols to transmit messages in Morse code. Until now, linguists have placed great emphasis on the formal components of utterances, but in so doing have generally neglected the cognitive complements that are an integral part of any act of written or spoken communication. It is the task of modern rhetoric to remind us that language was begotten by speech, and to demonstrate the importance of the cognitive memory and all the non-linguistic components in verbal communication. Theorizing on translation and interpretation offers the ideal vantage point for studying discourse.

If, for example, we adopt the second interpretation, then "The Icy Grip Tightens" embodies two ideas, that of "bitter cold" and that of "persistence," which carries a pejorative connotation whose source is "grip," the key word. In fact, meaning is not grasped in words, but in itself, independently of any signifier. It is solely for practical reasons that I have expressed it here in the form of key words accompanied by an explanation of their possible connotations.

In sum, to understand an utterance, one must draw the concepts out of the signifiers and link them to the world of experience by augmenting them with one's own non-linguistic knowledge. Language is only one of the components of a message. Understanding signifieds and understanding meaning cannot, however, be regarded as one continuous action: the value of signs within the system is as important as their reference to the outside world. In semantics it is therefore difficult to draw the line between logic and linguistics.[57] Nevertheless, it can be said that *signification is codified and tends to be static, while meaning is not codified and tends to be dynamic.* Interpretation is the operation by which comprehension is achieved. Indeed, *understanding and interpretation are one and the same*, for the reasoning involved in understanding is an internal hermeneutic dialogue.

In concluding, it should be noted that no interlinguistic comparisons have yet been made; the analysis has been strictly intra- and extra-linguistic.

Reformulation

Re-expression, which is the next step after comprehension, is the act of re-verbalizing concepts using the signifiers of another language. This mental process is probably still the least well understood, the most mysterious, and the most complicated to analyze. The ideas identified through interpretive analysis set off a chain of analogical reasoning in the translator's mind. However, it is not easy to probe the workings of that most fascinating of computers—infinitely more complex than the man-made "thinking"

---

57. See Mounin, *Les problèmes théoriques*, p. 163.

machines—as it reformulates ideas. But it can be said with certainty that the search for equivalents is much more than a simple effort of memory in which the translator scans a kind of internal dictionary for words corresponding to the concepts to be reconstituted. Reformulation is not a mere labelling of concepts. It is, fundamentally, an act of intelligence, a series of "living and acting operations,"[58] even if the translator is not conscious of each one.

To study the genesis of an idea, we must venture into obscure, little-known regions of the mind and try to follow the meandering progress of analogical thought. Attempting to imagine what happens once the signifiers have disappeared and the brain's non-linguistic mechanisms come into play is not an easy task. Alfred Binet's quip: "Thought is an unconscious activity of the mind,"[59] reminds us of the limitations of such an undertaking.

Although thought is abstract, it is based on speech. Thus, in reformulating ideas, the translator continually shuttles between the de-verbalized meaning seeking expression and the linguistic forms through which it could be verbalized. This back and forth motion finally ceases when a satisfactory match is made. Language and thought form a dialectical whole, or, as Slama-Cazacu says:

> The communication intention organizes the internal content and guides the speaker in the choice of a means of expression that will reflect not only the psychic content to be transmitted but also the parameters of the situation. This phenomenon of word choice, though simple and elementary in appearance, is in fact a complex process of thought and expression of relationships existing in the world.[60]

Analogical Reasoning

To discover the meaning of an utterance within a communication situation and re-express it in another language, the translator reasons by analogy, probing the expressive resources of the target language through a series of associations and deductions, or inferences. He progresses through several stages, but not necessarily in a straight line. "The mind is always free to detour," said Piaget. The human brain works by association, and the

---

58. Piaget, *The Psychology of Intelligence*, p. 7.

59. Cited in ibid., p. 29.

60. "En organisant le contenu intérieur, l'intention de communication imprime une direction dans le choix des moyens d'expression, en accord avec le contenu psychique qui doit être transmis, mais aussi avec tout le système de coordonnées de la situation donnée. Ce phénomène de choix des mots, simple et élémentaire en apparence, représente un processus complexe de réflexion et d'expression des rapports existants dans la réalité." Slama-Cazacu, *Langage et contexte*, pp. 169-70.

translator's competence depends to a large extent on his deductive and associative abilities.[61]

It is no coincidence that many professional translators find Paul Robert's *Dictionnaire alphabétique et analogique de la langue française* particularly well suited to their needs. The *Robert* has distinguished itself from other dictionaries by exploiting the associations between ideas. Every entry, according to the preface, contains as complete an inventory as possible of all kinds of *analogical relationships*, be they based on etymology, the terms used in the definitions, syntactic links, synonymy, antonymy, or any other of the multitude of threads that *logic weaves between words*.[62] The dictionary is analogical in that it allows the reader to trace words by their meaning and discover unknown words.[63] It is hardly an exaggeration to say that this excellent work tool is often a source of inspiration for the translator who, having grasped the meaning of a passage, must search for the thread that will lead him to the appropriate word or idiomatic expression in the target language. Although it might not always provide him with a solution, Robert's dictionary will at least help him to work his way out of a blind alley and steer him back onto a profitable course of analogical reasoning. The dictionary defines analogy as a similarity established by the imagination (and often confirmed in the language by the various senses of a given word) between two or more essentially different concepts. Under "analogy" can be found the related terms in French for "association," "correspondence," "link," "kinship," "relation," "relationship," and "induction."

Before analyzing the analogical process by which a French equivalent was found for "The Icy Grip Tightens," let us look at a simpler example, namely the "WORKING" indicator on an instant photo booth.[64] When the photo machine is *ready to go into operation again*, a green light goes on beside the "WORKING" sign. The user then has simply to sit down in the booth and insert a coin into the proper slot: the camera starts automatically. Literally, "WORKING" can mean either that the photo booth is in working order and thus ready to go into operation, or that it is actually *in* operation.

---

61. The primary purpose of a translation aptitude test should not be to evaluate the breadth of a candidate's vocabulary or even his knowledge of the risks of language interference in translation. Rather, it should be to test his aptitude for logical reasoning and his insight into the relationships between quantities or concepts. It would not be a matter of evaluating the subject's IQ (if, indeed, intelligence can be measured at all), but his ability to think. Such tests would have to be very carefully designed, for they could easily miss the mark and measure something other than what was intended. They nevertheless merit the attention of researchers in applied translatology. See "Qualities of the Translator," chapter 1, and "Preserving Textual Organicity," chapter 3.

62. Robert, *Dictionnaire alphabétique et analogique*, p. viii (my italics).

63. Ibid., p. ix.

64. Anecdote recounted by M. Lederer.

But "en marche," the faulty French translation given in this particular case, always means the latter. For example, one would say of a running motor that it is "en marche." In order to render the meaning of the English sign correctly, the translator must avoid the literal translation "en marche" and think the problem through; to do so he must take a circuitous route.

One often fruitful approach is by way of the negative. If the machine had been broken, what would have replaced the word "WORKING"? Perhaps "NOT WORKING," or, more idiomatically, "OUT OF ORDER" or "OUT OF SERVICE." A francophone would probably have written "EN PANNE," "HORS D'USAGE," or "HORS SERVICE." This last negative equivalent brings to mind the positive expression "EN SERVICE," which idiomatically renders the meaning of "WORKING" in the situation described (see Figure 2). In searching for an equivalent, the translator must often, though not always consciously, resort to analogical reasoning, either because the consecrated (and therefore obligatory) equivalent does not come to mind or, as we shall see later, because the translation equivalent can be found only by re-creating the context.[65] Analogical reasoning is a process by which the imagination establishes similarities. Analogy plays a very important part in the search for translation equivalents and indeed in the very workings of intelligence. Aspiring translators should therefore possess imagination and a sensitivity to parallels and connections between concepts in order to transfer the concepts contained in a text into another text.[66] There is a tendency to minimize the creative aspect of the cognitive process of translation, probably because such "second-hand" creation is deemed less noble than so-called original work. However, many original works are simply personal re-statements of thoughts already expressed. Anything re-stated is in fact a translation. Creation, interpretation, re-creation, translation, and adaptation are more closely related than one might think.

Re-verbalization

What goes on in the translator's mind as he searches for a French formulation corresponding to his interpretation of "The Icy Grip Tightens"? This is only a hypothesis, but let us suppose that after isolating the ideas of "bitter cold" and "persistence + pejorative connotation," he proceeds to explore, by analogy, the resources of the target language in search of linguistic signs capable of rendering those ideas. Of the many paths he could follow, let us

---

65. See chapter 3, "Retrieval of Standard Equivalents from the Linguistic System," and "Re-Creation in Context."
66. Is it possible to measure an individual's creative potential, his powers of imagination? It appears that the makers of intelligence tests have just begun to take an interest in that aspect of intelligence. The theory of translation could well benefit from an attempt to evaluate, as accurately as possible, the role played by imagination in proposing message equivalents.

Figure 2
Simple Analogical Program

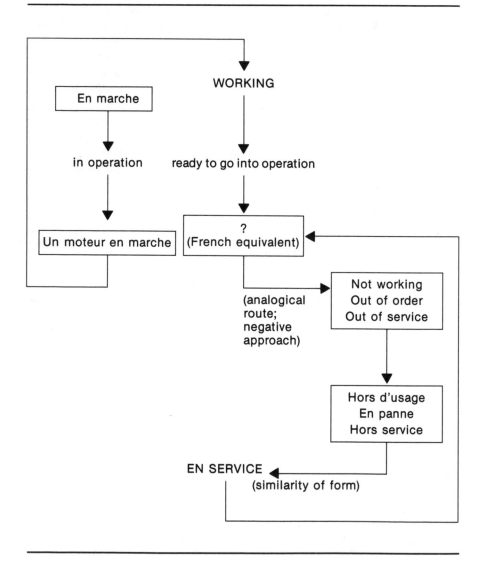

pursue one. Scanning his memory for signs coinciding with the idea of "bitter cold," as if he were searching through an encyclopedia, he might have summoned up,[67] or activated at a subconscious level, solutions like "très grand froid," "froid de canard," "froid à pierre fendre," "froid de loup," and "morsure du froid." Like a computer rejecting an inappropriate command, he immediately would have set them aside for linguistic or referential reasons. The expression "morsure du froid," however, might have evoked the verb "ne pas démordre," which might in turn have called up the verbs "s'entêter," "ne pas lâcher prise," and "s'obstiner," all of which render the idea of "persistence + negative connotation." On reflecting on the "froid mordant" and "ne pas démordre" combination, the translator may have intuitively perceived another analogy and become vaguely aware of a possible solution to his problem. He might then have tried to articulate those basic elements in a properly structured sentence. Perhaps he mentally produced tentative equivalents such as "Le froid mordant persiste" or "Le froid ne démord pas."

While this particular chain of analogies is probable, it is only conjecture. One thing, however, is certain: *once the meaning has been grasped, it is reformulated by means of ideas, and not of words.* Consciously and subconsciously, the translator gropes for a suitable formulation. Information is summoned or evoked from the memory. Each time the translator, in the course of this exploration, rejects a possible solution as unsatisfactory, he is passing judgement on the appropriateness of its form and content. In fact, the translator's reasoning is creative; he is engaging in the cognitive process by which general knowledge, or all the linguistic and encyclopedic information stored in the brain, is brought into play.

Another translator could presumably have followed some other path, arriving at either the identical solution (a not improbable outcome), or a different one (a more probable outcome). The same interpretation can be expressed in different ways in the target language, as long as the target-language signifiers are not dictated by usage, as is the case with codified languages. Some equivalents are fixed. For example, "Old Testament" can only be translated by "Ancien Testament." Thus, the greater the predominance of set forms in a given field, the less liberty the translator has to re-express ideas related to that field: he must comply with the accepted usage.

---

67. "While the rational organization of the encyclopedia allows for information to be *summoned* with the concept it is related to, symbolic organization allows for information to be *evoked* from other information associated with it." ("Tandis que l'organisation rationnelle de l'encyclopédie permet de *convoquer* directement une information à partir du concept dont elle relève, l'organisation symbolique permet *d'évoquer* une information à partir d'autres informations auxquelles elle est associée." Sperber, "Rudiments de rhétorique cognitive," p. 404 (Sperber's italics).

Sometimes an equivalent is discovered quite spontaneously. Inspiration strikes, and concepts are instantly matched. This happens when a perfect understanding of the ideas to be rendered is combined with a perfect command of the linguistic means available to express them. What has been properly grasped is easily re-expressed, and the richer the translator's palette, the more colourful will be his rendition of the original. In other cases, however, reformulation is a more laborious process. Sometimes the mind has to be coaxed into producing an acceptable equivalent: analogies must be "induced" and trains of thought more consciously followed.

Verification

The purpose of verification, the third and final stage of the cognitive process of translation, is to confirm the accuracy of the solution. This is done by checking that the proposed equivalent perfectly renders the full meaning of the original utterance. Let us first see how, in context, "Le froid ne démord pas" can be justified as an equivalent for "The Icy Grip Tightens."

In French, the negative form of the verb *démordre* is used figuratively in a pejorative sense to mean that a person is "as stubborn as a mule." This usage renders the *idea* of "persistence + pejorative connotation" that was extracted during the interpretation of the original statement. The paralyzing cold, "qui ne lâchait pas prise," has made Americans prisoners in their own homes. "Démordre" also evokes "froid mordant" and "morsure du froid" (both meaning "biting cold")—metaphorical expressions for "froid rigoureux" ("bitter cold"). The figurative meaning of "ne pas démordre" is superimposed on the figurative meaning of "mordre" as applied to "froid" ("cold"). This sort of pun is very common in advertising and journalism. It is often used in the creation of slogans or banners splashed across advertisements to attract the reader's attention. Newspaper and magazine headlines serve much the same purpose. For all of these linguistic and para-linguistic reasons, then, "Le froid ne démord pas" can be considered, not the best or only translation possible, but an acceptable *functional equivalent* of "The Icy Grip Tightens," given the way the title has been interpreted.

What can we learn from the foregoing analysis? What insights does it give us into the process of verification? It demonstrates two things: first, that verification is always a function of the interpretation that preceded re-expression; and second, that verification is itself a form of interpretation.

In verifying his translation, the translator attempts to determine to what extent his reformulation matches the meaning of the original passage, or to be more precise, his interpretation of the author's intent. An objectively erroneous interpretation can give rise to a subjectively logical verification. Anyone who has taught translation knows how passionately and persistently some students can insist on interpreting a passage in their own way. It requires immense tact to bring students like this around to admitting that their version is incongruous, especially when the instructor cannot cite linguistic or factual proof. A preference for one equivalent over another can be due to individual sensitivity or to a certain intuitive perception that cannot be rationally explained. As was pointed out earlier, translation is an *art* of re-expression.

In any case, as far as the translation process is concerned, the important fact is that, whether his first interpretation is correct or not, the translator goes back through the same steps that initially led to his trial solution. The cognitive process is the same in both cases; only the signifiers are different. In our example, we analyzed the signification of "ne pas démordre" and "mordre" to confirm that they were appropriate, not in relation to the words of the original utterance, whose form they do not resemble, but in relation to the ideas extracted from the message during the first interpretation. Words are never translated; the meaning underlying them is.

Verification is, in fact, a second interpretation. The first interpretation takes place after the concepts have been understood and before they are re-expressed; its purpose is to identify the ideas in the message. The second interpretation takes place after re-expression and before selection of the final version; its purpose is to determine whether the signifiers of the tentative solution accurately convey the ideas of the message. This quality check on the translation is also a reasoning process. Translating thus entails two interpretations—the first based on the signs of the source text, the second based on the signs of the target language once the tentative solution or possible equivalents have been proposed. In both cases, the sole object of the interpretation is meaning. The cognitive process is illustrated in Figure 3 (see also Figures 1 and 4).

Figure 3
The Two Phases of Interpretation in the Translation Process
(Semasiological and Onomasiological)

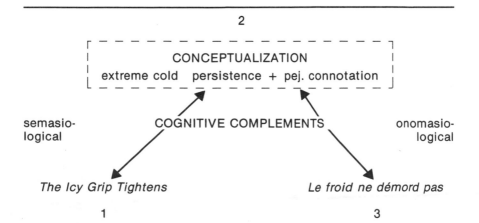

In both cases the vectors representing the interpretive analysis pass through the prism of non-linguistic knowledge. The vectors point in both directions because during the interpretive analysis the translator continually moves back and forth between the signifiers of the source language and the concepts they suggest (first interpretation), and then between those concepts and the target-language signifiers that best express them (second interpretation).

From this analysis of the cognitive mechanisms underlying translation, it is clear that the comparison of languages plays no role in verification, or in any other stage. The translator does not place the signs of the source language side by side with those of the target language in order to note similarities or differences, as the student of comparative stylistics does. Instead, *he constantly adapts the expressive potential of words to the rhetorical framework of the message.* In this sense the translator is a technician: he does not deal with language in the abstract, but with language use. In comparative stylistics the main interest lies in describing the base of the triangle shown in Figure 3, and the investigation is essentially limited to fixed forms of language. Contrastive linguistics is a valuable pedagogical tool for studying mandatory or standard equivalences, but it is incapable of describing the cognitive and rhetorical processes involved in translation. If the translator returns to the original text during the verification phase, it is because he is not really sure whether his first interpretation was accurate and complete. Once again he analyzes each meaning element in the original and in his reformulation to ensure that both carry the same denotation and connotation, because both must fulfil the same intent. That is why only an analytical method can produce equivalent messages.

Figure 4 summarizes, in diagram form, the steps involved in the heuristic process of translation. The process starts and ends with a text. The translator subjects segments of the text—successive utterances of discourse—to interpretation during the comprehension and verification stages. He does not, however, analyze the segments in isolation, but with reference to a structured, meaningful whole: the text (see p. 102). The translator's goal is to construct a second text that performs the same communication function as the original text.

THE COMPARATIVE METHOD

Vinay and Darbelnet's *Stylistique comparée* is one of the richest works ever produced on the classification and description of the differences and similarities between two languages. To a large extent it applies the categories of internal stylistics—especially those of Charles Bally—and the procedures of classical rhetoric in a methodical and innovative comparison of French and

Figure 4
Heuristics of Translation

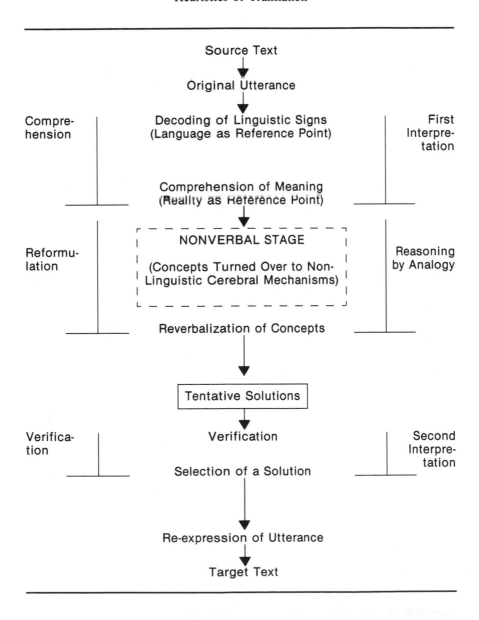

English. These external stylistics are developed on three levels: the lexicon, the organization (morphology and syntax) of thought, and the message (which is understood essentially as being the sum of the significations in an utterance). This is a descriptive discipline, which, Vinay and Darbelnet maintain, falls within the province of linguistics.

According to the authors, the comparative method has applications in three areas: academic translation (to test comprehension), professional translation (to communicate), and linguistic research (to make observations).[68] For students of a foreign language, the comparison of two linguistic systems can be a method of acquiring and testing linguistic knowledge. For apprentice translators, the method is supposed to improve comprehension of the techniques used in moving from one language to another and to facilitate systematic examination of the text to be translated by identifying difficulties. For researchers, the comparison of two languages is an investigative tool that enables one to "observe how one language functions in relation to another" and "to shed light on phenomena that would otherwise remain invisible."[69] There are several comments to be made about the application of the comparative method to the teaching of professional translation.

The Categories of "Stylistique comparée"

The pairs of equivalents analyzed, described, and catalogued by the comparatists are drawn from two sources: (1) the language as code (structural meaning) and (2) translated texts, elements of which are extracted and often dealt with out of context. Comparatists do not distinguish between equivalent words or sentences and equivalent messages in establishing the taxonomic categories of comparative stylistics. A few examples of these categories, at each of the three levels of analysis, are given below:

	English	*French*
	LEXICON	
particularization and generalization	bus	autobus, car
intellectual sense vs. emotional sense	belligerent (at war) vs. belligerent (warlike)	belligérent belliqueux
false cognates	actual	actuel
lexical modulation (e.g., means vs. end)	firewood	bois de chauffage

---

68.   Vinay and Darbelnet, *Stylistique comparée*, p. 24.
69.   ". . . observer le fonctionnement d'une langue par rapport à une autre"; "éclairer certains phénomènes qui, sans elle, resteraient ignorés." Ibid., p. 25.

MORPHOLOGY AND SYNTAX

transposition (adverb/verb)	He will soon be back.	Il ne tardera pas à rentrer.
chassé-croisé	blown away	emporté par le vent
categories		
—plural words translated by singular words	the stairs	l'escalier
—singular words translated by plural words	glass	vitraux
ellipsis	He did not say.	Il ne l'a pas dit.
verb tense, voice and aspect of verbs, etc.		

MESSAGE

structural false cognates	a man of the people	un homme du peuple
dilution	the balance sheet	le bilan
concentration	archery	le tir à l'arc
economy of words	previously unpublished	inédit
turns of phrase	some people think	il y a des gens qui pensent
emphasis (e.g., by repetition)	yes, indeed	oui, oui
modulation (e.g., concrete vs. abstract)	And I don't mean maybe.	Et je ne plaisante pas.
gain, loss, etc.		

The categories of comparative stylistics effectively describe the pairs of equivalents chosen by the authors. But of the many equivalents imaginable for any given word, syntagma, or utterance, the comparatists fasten on a single one. Thus, "from cover to cover" rendered as "de la première à la dernière page" is cited as an example of lexical modulation characterized by a change of comparison.[70] This observation is certainly true of that particular pair of equivalents, but within a given context (and even in the language itself without reference to any particular text), there are other functional solutions, equally valid *from the translator's point of view*, that could render the same idea: "Il a lu le livre du début à la fin"; "Il a lu le livre en entier"; "Il a lu tout le livre"; "Il a lu le livre au complet"; "Il a lu le livre de A à Z." Out of context, the original phrase simply means "He has read the whole book." The translator could have many different reasons for choosing one solution over another, for example, to avoid repetition, to reproduce a stylistic effect, or to compensate for a loss. Further-

---

70. Vinay and Darbelnet, *Stylistique comparée*, p. 90.

more, as part of a communicative situation, the utterance could have an altogether unexpected meaning, as was the case with "smooth" in the example analyzed earlier.

The categories of comparative stylistics are derived from the equivalents chosen; hence their contingent nature. Indeed, this is inevitable, because Vinay and Darbelnet study "signs divorced from messages" (as is clear from the previously mentioned categories), citing "practical and pedagogical reasons"[71] to justify their approach. This methodological bias is quite legitimate from a linguistic point of view. From the point of view of translation, however, it has the unfortunate effect of lending too much importance to the formal and contingent aspect of linguistic signs at the expense of the meaning that they carry in discourse. Discourse analysis is the basis of any real translation. The linguistic analysis practised in comparative stylistics falls short of discourse analysis and can lead to it only indirectly.

The Translation "Procedures"

Vinay and Darbelnet's seven technical translation procedures are among the most renowned categories of the comparative method.[72] But are they really "procedures"? Do they help the translator find translation equivalents? A procedure is a method used to obtain a result, a way of doing something, of carrying an activity through to its conclusion. But these "procedures" are in fact labels attached to results; the authors describe structural changes that occur in the translation process, or point out what does not change. To say that Vinay and Darbelnet's procedures are of any help in establishing contextual equivalences is to confuse the ends and the means. The term "procedure" is misleading, because *comparative stylistics does not study the process by which equivalences are established, but rather describes the characteristics of selected pairs of equivalents.*

The translator has a certain amount of leeway in choosing the linguistic means by which to re-express a message. This is a relative but creative freedom that comparatists would not deny. Cases in which only one solution is possible are therefore rare, with the exception of "compulsory" equivalents dictated by usage. Consequently, one statement in the source language can be rendered by various formulations in the target language, each of which is arrived at through a different "procedure." Because it is impossible to predict which will be used, the procedures are of no operational value in semantic transfer. Facilitating neither the analysis of a message nor its reconstruction, they cannot rightfully be called practical rules of translation.

---

71. Ibid., p. 29.
72. Loan word, calque, literal translation, transposition, modulation, equivalence, and adaptation. (Loan words are not translated, and calques are simply transcoded.)

I have no quarrel with the observation that the translation of "grown wearisome from constant repetition" by "qui finit par lasser à force d'être répété" involves a triple transposition: adjective/verb, adjective/adverbial phrase, and noun/verb.[73] However, even if he were able to infer it, this observation would be of no practical use to the translator seeking to render "grown wearisome from constant repetition" in French. Indeed, the information that one adjective in the utterance was to become a verb, another was to turn into an adverbial phrase, and the noun was also to be replaced by a verb would be of little interest to him because he would still have no way of knowing *which* verbs, or *which* adverbial phrase. He would know the form but not the content. The linguistic analysis carried out after the fact in comparative stylistics bears no relation to the cognitive process of translation. Ljudskanov says that "Most proponents of that approach analyze translation only as a *result*, that is, in a prescriptive fashion, even though they regard it in principle as a linguistic process."[74]

It is therefore clear that the categories of comparative stylistics (and particularly the so-called translation procedures) cannot really be applied to the analysis and re-expression of messages, or even the verification of equivalences. Establishing after the fact that there has been a "transfer," a "modulation," or an "adaptation" in no way guarantees that the translation will accurately render the meaning of the original. Vinay and Darbelnet's procedures, therefore, cannot be regarded as translation algorithms. If they could, verifying the accuracy of a translation would simply be a matter of applying the appropriate algorithm, just as one applies grammatical rules to check the agreement of verb and subject. Only *interpretation* can bridge the gap between language and discourse.

In order to compare, one must have a point of comparison. In comparative stylistics, the original utterance is placed side by side with an equivalent (usually transcoded) in the target language. But the translator has only one side of the equation at his disposal: the source text, composed of a series of interdependent utterances. He cannot very well compare an utterance in one language with an as-yet unformulated equivalent in another language. His task is precisely to give form to that equivalent, and we have already seen by what process he achieves his goal. In fact, it is up to him to find the second point that makes comparison possible. Comparative stylistics

---

73. Vinay and Darbelnet, *Stylistique comparée*, p. 97.
74. "La plupart des représentants de cette conception analysent la traduction seulement en tant que *résultat* donné, c'est-à-dire d'une manière normative bien qu'ils affirment en principe que c'est un processus linguistique." Ljudskanov, *Traduction humaine*, vol. 1, p. 44 (Ljudskanov's italics).

short-circuits the interpretive process of translation; its categories, therefore, cannot be regarded as translation rules or procedures.[75]

These criticisms do not detract from the contribution of comparative stylistics to the science of language. As long as translation is considered an operation carried out on language, the authors are right. Although accurate in its analysis of the fixed forms and phrases particular to each language, the comparative method can only theoretically be applied to discourse. In order to deal with texts, which are instances of discourse, one must go further. Vinay and Darbelnet are correct in saying that the French equivalent of "All Buses Must Stop Here" is "Arrêt obligatoire des autobus." They cannot, however, predict anything that is not already set down in the language system. *The translator creates new phrases.* That is why linguistics, if it is to explain the translation process fully, must first undertake to study discourse and its relation to thought and communication.

The Contribution of Comparative Stylistics

Although the authors of *Stylistique comparée* erred in presenting their work as a "method of translation" and setting forth a posteriori observations as a priori rules, they have made an extremely important contribution. They have shown that the differences between languages cannot be fully catalogued in terms of phonetics, lexical semantics, morphology, syntax and, generally, the functioning of linguistic signs, because members of different language communities use different linguistic equipment to express their thoughts and feelings. In other words, each community has developed habits of expression that, over time, have been integrated into the language and lent it certain characteristics. This insight is of primary importance to translation for, as Edmond Cary said, "what truly distinguishes translation is that it takes place in the context of the relations between two cultures, two worlds of thought and perception." The best pages of *Stylistique comparée* are those devoted to the "characterology," or "personality profile," of English and French. Applied to languages, characterology is, according to Darbelnet, the study of the traits that characterize an idiom, that is, the study of the nature and use of the lexical, syntactic, and prosodic resources of a language. As he himself puts it, these are "the tools, the apparatus with which languages have equipped themselves over the years to meet the needs of their speakers. Those

---

75. "Contrastive linguistics (by that or any other name, such as 'comparative grammar' or 'comparative stylistics') is often portrayed, falsely, as a science of translation, when in fact it is only a product of it." ("La linguistique contrastive [qu'elle apparaisse sous ce nom ou sous ceux de 'grammaire comparée,' 'stylistique comparée,' etc.] tend à s'ériger abusivement en science de la traduction, dont elle n'est en fait que le produit.") Pergnier, "Traduction et théorie linguistique," p. 29.

needs appear to vary, in both nature and intensity, from one language to another." He adds: "two languages can both be inflected and belong to the same family yet nevertheless differ considerably in the way they express ideas and convey emotions."[76] By taking a broader perspective than the comparison of words or syntactic structures, the authors discovered, more by intuition than by scientific observation (a weakness that linguists have not failed to point out)[77] certain traits characteristic of English and of French. These general tendencies exhibited by languages, which are by no means absolute, help to guide the translator as he crosses from one language to another.[78] Though linguists[79] dispute (from a strictly linguistic point of view) the validity of Vinay and Darbelnet's observations on the characteristics of French and English, these are, nevertheless, the most innovative feature of the book and, it is safe to say, a major reason for its resounding and well-deserved success.

Some of the practical exercises that I developed for teaching English-to-French translation (in the original French version of this book) were inspired by Vinay and Darbelnet's observations. Since the observations are related to the concerns of bilingual discourse analysis, they are well suited to a method based on writing techniques and the manipulation of language. For example, I constructed exercises to illustrate the preference of French for noun forms and of English for verbal constructions, and the use in English of co-ordination and juxtaposition where French prefers subordination and articulation, always, however, drawing on texts or portions of texts that provide a sufficient context for interpreting meaning. Other exercises for training translators were based on the use of deixis and the tendency of English to describe the world in comparative rather than absolute terms.

In general, then, *Stylistique comparée* is primarily an instrument for observing how two linguistic systems function; it is not a true method of

---

76. ". . . l'outillage, l'équipement dont les langues se sont dotées au cours de leur histoire pour satisfaire les besoins de ceux qui les parlent. Or, apparemment, ces besoins, de par leur nature et leur intensité, varient d'une langue à l'autre . . . . deux langues peuvent être toutes les deux flexionnelles, appartenir à la même famille et n'en présenter pas moins des caractères différents dans leur façon d'exprimer les idées et les mouvements de la sensibilité." Darbelnet, "Caractérologie linguistique," p. 1.

77. In his review of *Stylistique comparée*, Mounin expresses reservations about Vinay and Darbelnet's "intuitive and subjective" method, which lacks the rigour of a statistical analysis. He points out that "The book, which contains so many excellent and thought-provoking examples, also illustrates this defect: when examples are not *counted*, they are always selected, sometimes constructed, and sometimes distorted to support the thesis." ("Ce livre, si riche d'exemples excellents pour faire réfléchir au problème, illustre aussi cette lacune : les exemples, quand ils ne sont pas *comptés*, sont toujours choisis, quelquefois construits, quelquefois distordus, pour aller dans le sens de la thèse.") *Linguistique et traduction*, p. 233 (Mounin's italics).

78. Differences between French and English have also been pointed out by Duron in *Langue française, langue humaine*.

79. Georges Mounin and Mario Wandruszka in particular.

translation. In the introduction the authors themselves say:

> By comparing French with English we have been able to discern characteristics of French and, through contrast, characteristics of English that would be invisible to a linguist studying only one language. When it is used not to understand or to communicate but rather to observe how one language works compared with another, translation becomes an *investigative process*. It sheds light on phenomena that would otherwise have remained hidden. As such, translation is a *subsidiary discipline of linguistics*.[80]

This passage speaks for itself, and it is significant that Vinay felt compelled to include it in his review of developments in translation theory over two decades in a special issue of *Meta* (1975).[81] It confirms the fact that when Vinay speaks of translation, he clearly means the translation of a language, not of a text. "How do you translate English (or French)?" is the basic question that *Stylistique comparée* asks, not "How do you translate this English text into French?" By its very nature a text comprises more than fixed expressions, and if a translation is to reflect the genius of the language, the equivalents cannot all be determined in advance. The translation of language must therefore not be confused with the translation of texts. *The translation of language is an exercise in comparison, the translation of texts, an exercise in interpretation.*

With few exceptions the two workbooks accompanying *Stylistique comparée* are made up of exercises in the transcoding of words, syntagmas, or sentences, and their purpose, as the authors themselves say, is to facilitate the study of French and English. The workbooks are designed for "francophones who wish to specialize in English [and] for those who simply wish to improve their command of their mother tongue"; "bilingualism inevitably confuses two structural and stylistic systems."[82] The epigraph[83] to the first

---

80. "La comparaison du français et de l'anglais nous a permis de dégager du français, et par voie de contraste, de l'anglais, des caractères qui resteraient invisibles au linguiste travaillant sur une seule langue. Il semble donc que la traduction, non pour comprendre ni pour faire comprendre, mais pour observer le fonctionnement d'une langue par rapport à une autre, soit un *procédé d'investigation*. Elle permet d'éclaircir certains phénomènes qui sans elle resteraient ignorés. À ce titre elle est une *discipline auxiliaire de la linguistique*." Vinay and Darbelnet, *Stylistique comparée*, p. 25 (my italics).

81. Vinay, "Regards sur l'évolution des théories," pp. 7-27.

82. ". . . aux francophones qui désirent se spécialiser en anglais [ou à] ceux qui cherchent avant tout à mieux pratiquer les ressources de leur langue maternelle"; "le bilinguisme entraîne inévitablement le mélange des deux systèmes structuraux et stylistiques," Vinay and Darbelnet, *Cahier d'exercice n° 1*, Avertissement, p. ix.

83. "English, if we learn it well enough to master its nuances, will help us defend our own language. It will give us an opportunity to rid French of the vagueness that saps its strength: if we are able to recognize anglicisms, we can avoid them. Today English is displacing French as the result of faulty translations ingrained in the language." ("L'anglais, poursuivi jusque dans ses nuances, nous aidera donc aussi à défendre notre langue. Nous y trouverons une occasion de plus de bannir l'à peu près qui nous ronge; connaissant l'anglicisme, nous le fuirons. Aujourd'hui, l'anglais gagne sur le français par suite des traductions incorrectes qui s'incrustent.") Édouard Montpetit, *La Conquête économique*, cited as epigraph to Vinay and Darbelnet's *Cahier d'exercice n° 1*.

workbook is indicative of the need that *Stylistique comparée* filled and continues to fill: in Canada, French is strongly influenced, if not contaminated, by English. Knowing the historical and social context in which the comparative method was conceived provides an insight into the basic attitudes underlying it. Comparative stylistics is an ideal technique for comparing two linguistic competences—French and English—and an excellent preparation for learning translation in the true sense. It might even be said that *one must learn how to translate language correctly, a task for which the comparative method is well suited, before one can translate texts.*

An example should make clear the difference between comparing transcoded equivalents and interpreting meaning in order to propose a contextual equivalent. A good method for improving one's command of English is to compare expressions such as "there is no such thing as" and "there is nothing like." Although similar in form, the two expressions have very different meanings, the first signifying "does not exist" ("There are no such things as ghosts": "Les fantômes n'existent pas"), the second, "nothing is better than" ("There's nothing like a good meal!": "Il n'y a rien de tel qu'un bon repas!/Rien ne vaut un bon repas!/Rien n'est plus agréable qu'un bon repas!"). This distinction in meaning exists in language, but does not always exist in discourse. In discourse, it is even possible for "there is nothing like" to mean "does not exist"—the sense that in language is usually attributed to "there is no such thing as." The following example, taken from Stephen Ullmann's *Semantics*,[84] is an illustration: "*There is certainly nothing* like an automatic connexion between the interest which a subject commands and the number of metaphors inspired by it." In French this is translated by: "*Il n'existe sûrement aucune* corrélation directe entre l'intérêt suscité par une réalité et le nombre de métaphores qu'elle inspire." Here the transcoded and contextual equivalents do not match at all, striking proof that, *more frequently than is usually realized, the context alters the meaning generally ascribed to the words and expressions of a given linguistic system taken out of context.* As a result, while it is important for the translator to *learn*, by the comparative method, the distinction between "there is no such thing as" and "there is nothing like," it is equally important for him to *understand* the meaning of these expressions when they are used in context. If he does not, he will translate by rote.

Georges Mounin was correct when he said that the ambition of general linguistics and applied linguistics (such as *Stylistique comparée*, used as an "investigative tool") is "less to train [translators] than to inform them; less to teach them their art or transform that art into an infallible science than to provide them with a broader general knowledge of language phenomena as a guide."[85]

---

84. Ullmann, *Semantics*, p. 202 (my italics).
85. ". . . moins de les former que de les informer; moins de leur enseigner leur art, ou de transformer cet art en science infaillible, que de leur fournir sur les phénomènes du langage une culture générale plus large et plus complète, qui les éclaire." Mounin, *Linguistique et traduction*, pp. 86-87.

If the act of translation is to be properly defined, the part of the translator's competence that stems from knowledge of languages pure and simple must be clearly separated from the part that has to do with the interpretive process. Unless this distinction is made, the process of translation in context is distorted into a simple search for formal equivalents. Because translation is an analysis of discourse rather than a comparison of two languages, the teaching of translation cannot be reduced solely to comparative exercises. Translation is not comparison.

Comparative Stylistics and Translation Teaching

Without question, comparative stylistics has a place in a program of translator training. However, it is primarily a method for bilinguals to improve their command of their two languages. It has a role to play in the pedagogy of translation because, despite the admission requirements of translation schools, student translators' knowledge of languages is often less than perfect. The advantage of the comparative method is that it brings out the structural differences between two languages and the differences in how the languages dissect reality. It reveals the distinct characterological traits of each language. For student translators, it may be considered the final step in learning a second language and a means of consolidating their command of the first language. In this sense, comparative stylistics is a sub-discipline of translation, just as lexicology, general linguistics, and terminology are. It should thus be taught early in the program because knowledge of languages is a prerequisite to the practice of translation. It is pedagogically unsound to postpone comparative stylistics to the end of the program.

Translation involves more than the comparison of two linguistic codes, and, as a result, the goals of an introductory translation course are not the same as those of a course in comparative stylistics. The comparison of languages cannot be the subject matter of practical instruction in translation. *In comparative stylistics the approach is descriptive and prescriptive, whereas in translation it is interpretive and communicative.* The first approach belongs to linguistics, the second, to discourse analysis—the discipline (not yet widely known) that combines the study of discourse (rhetoric) with communication science. The classification of structural transformations into comparative categories cannot bridge the gap between language analysis and discourse analysis.

Paradoxically, it is a model of unilingual communication that best explains the translation process, because translation is in fact a particular form of interpersonal communication. In using language to communicate, one associates words with ideas, which is precisely what the translator does in translating. This is why "the foreign language [is] an obstacle to be overcome rather than an object to be translated"[86]—or compared. Any attempt to introduce a comparative approach—which has no place in discourse analysis—distorts the process.[87]

CONCLUSION

Because the semiotic, linguistic, sociolinguistic, and comparative approaches have all failed to provide a comprehensive explanation of the translation process, it is clear that no general theory of translation exists, that is, none that has taken the interpretation of meaning as its object.[88] This theoretical deficiency could in part account for the still-experimental nature of translation pedagogy and the difficulties encountered by those who have attempted to develop a systematic approach.

Having reached an impasse by pursuing linguistic theories that all but ignore the meaning of utterances, linguists now seem to be turning toward the study of communicative situations, of presuppositions—in short, toward discourse analysis. Such work in applied linguistics, a healthy reaction to Chomsky's generative grammar, is currently at the forefront of linguistic research, and translation theory will undoubtedly benefit from this renewed interest in meaning.[89] Indeed, it seems that any systematic study of translation pedagogy must focus on the actualization of signs and on the referential

---

86.   "La langue étrangère [est] un obstacle à surmonter plutôt qu'un objet à traduire." Lederer, "Synecdoque et traduction," p. 39.

87.   "If the translator's art is essentially to dissociate languages by taking meaning as the object of translation . . . , then it is clear that by introducing language comparisons one is in effect posing false problems." ("Si l'art essentiel de la traduction consiste à dissocier des langues en prenant le sens comme objet à traduire . . . on comprend que faire intervenir en traduction des comparaisons de langue revienne à poser de faux problèmes.") Lederer, "La traduction," p. 24.

88.   "Philosophy and art explore the boundaries of meaning and communication; linguistics sets out the formal parameters of utterances; the translator, who is responsible for ensuring that communication takes place, must take meaning as his object and define that meaning as what the author intended to say." ("Il appartient à la philosophie et à l'art d'explorer les limites du sens et du communicable, à la linguistique de déterminer les paramètres formels de l'énoncé; quant au traducteur, qui se doit d'assurer la communication, il lui faut définir son objet comme étant le sens, et celui-ci comme étant le vouloir dire de l'auteur.") Ibid., p. 16.

89.   In a lecture given at the University of Ottawa, Igor Melchuk argued that "advances in practical translation are of greater importance to linguistics than advances in linguistics are to the practice of translation." ("Les conquêtes en traduction pratique sont plus importantes pour la linguistique que les conquêtes en linguistique ne le sont pour la pratique de la traduction.") He developed this point in an article entitled "Théorie de langage, théorie de traduction," where he also said that "the science of translation, as distinct from, and even to some extent opposed to, linguistics, does not exist: linguistics *is* the science of translation." ("La science de la traduction, comme science séparée de la linguistique et même, dans un certain degré [*sic*], opposée à celle-ci, n'existe pas : la linguistique EST la science de la traduction.") "Théorie de langage," p. 296. This assertion is somewhat dogmatic; of which linguistics does he speak?

and situational, rather than the strictly linguistic, traits of that actualization. In order to explain the translation process fully, linguists must push their investigation beyond the signification of words to tackle discourse and its relationship with thought. Seleskovitch points out that "It is by observing human communication, not by describing languages, that we will develop a theory of translation."[90] This is so because the laws of language analysis do not correspond with the laws of discourse analysis.

In a translation course, it is more useful to teach students to use language than to pass on to them theoretical information about language. The translator is a language technician, not a linguist. We must follow UNESCO's lead in acknowledging "the principle that translation is an autonomous discipline that must be taught separately from language per se and requires specialized training."[91] Without going so far as to eliminate all theoretical courses from the curriculum, it is important to ensure that they do not encroach upon the students' training in the manipulation of language. In translation, theoretical knowledge is useful only to the extent that it serves as a basis for reflecting upon the practice of a technique.

Linguistics is to translation what physics is to biology. Medicine is not as advanced as physics because its object—the human being, complete with intelligence, emotions, unpredictable psychological reactions, and psychosomatic ailments—is more complex. In the same way, translation theory lags behind linguistics because its object—meaning, as it emerges from individual acts of uttering—eludes the precise descriptions of linguistic science.[92] There is unanimous agreement among linguists that semantics is the most difficult branch of their discipline to define systematically, for the descriptive methods used in grammar and phonology cannot be applied. Linguistics, as the science of language, is therefore physical, while translation, as an operation on discourse, is biological. A specific theory of translation, if it is to be compatible with a comprehensive approach to language as an instrument of human communication, must: (1) take the meaning of messages as its object; (2) deal not only with language, but also with discourse; and (3) explain the process of translation as well as its result.

A functional method of teaching translation cannot be based on signs divorced from messages, any more than a theory of translation can be. Instead, the method of instruction must, like the translator's intellectual processes, focus on the analysis of meaning. This is because the process of

---

90. "C'est en observant la communication humaine et non en décrivant les langues que l'on élaborera la théorie de la traduction." Seleskovitch, "Vision du monde et traduction," p. 107.
91. UNESCO "Draft Recommendation," p. 4.
92. "Language is more than acquired knowledge. It reflects the soul, the very humanity of the speaker." ("La langue est plus qu'un savoir acquis. Elle est liée à l'être, au caractère humain de celui qui parle.") Cary, *La traduction dans le monde moderne*, p. 8.

interpretive translation has much in common with the process of thought itself. Indeed, it is impossible to "dissociate the translating operation from mental operations in general; on the contrary, study of the normal functioning of language seems to open up more fruitful avenues of research into translation than does comparison of languages."[93]

Learning to translate professionally means learning to think and write well so as to effectively re-express in another language a written message transmitted within a given communication situation: nothing less. The translator must be particularly adept at analyzing the articulation of thought in discourse, that is, at subordinating linguistic forms to ideas. Translation pedagogy, approached from the point of view of discourse analysis, must therefore concentrate on the manipulation of language. That will be the topic of the next chapter.

---

93. ". . . dissocier l'opération traduction des opérations mentales en général; au contraire, l'étude du fonctionnement normal du langage nous semble ouvrir à la recherche sur la traduction des horizons plus fructueux que ceux que lui offre la comparaison des langues." Lederer, "La traduction : transcoder ou réexprimer?" p. 24.

CHAPTER 3

Levels of Language Manipulation

In chapter 2 I showed that translating is essentially an operation on discourse, and that discourse mediates between language and thought. It follows that the general objective of practical courses in translation should not be to describe languages (even if the description is comparative), but to analyze the ways in which thoughts are articulated in a message and can be reformulated in another language. The introductory course should focus on the use of language, devoting less attention to the result of the translation process than to the means by which that result is obtained. Discovering the principles of language manipulation should take precedence over examining individual cases.

But what exactly is the "manipulation of language"? In answering this question, we will be defining the proper focus of any method of translation teaching. We have already seen that the manipulation of language requires the dual skills of comprehension (to extract the author's intended meaning from the original text [interpretive analysis]) and re-expression (to reconstruct the text in another language [writing techniques]). Two complementary aptitudes—for interpretation and for expression—are therefore needed.

The disadvantage of this definition, from a pedagogical point of view, is that it is too general to enable a teacher to structure practical courses systematically. A more fruitful approach would take as its starting point the fact that all parts of discourse do not receive the same treatment in the establishment of translation equivalences. Four different levels of language manipulation can be distinguished:

1. observing conventions of form
2. performing interpretive analysis
    a) transfer of monosemous terms
    b) retrieval of standard equivalents from the linguistic system
    c) re-creation in context
3. interpreting style
4. preserving textual organicity

In describing these four levels, I shall draw on the first paragraph of the article "Rebuilding the Breast" for examples. This text was used in chapter 2 to demonstrate how analysis of the context could free a translation from blind compliance with dictionary significations. The original and its translation are reproduced below.

Rebuilding the Breast

After the removal of her left breast because of cancer in 1970, Mrs Joan Dawson, 54, of New York City, spent the next three years battling depression and a sense of loss. Then she decided to do something about it. Most women in the same situation turn to a psychiatrist. Mrs Dawson (not her real name) went to her doctor and asked him to rebuild her missing breast. "I didn't want to be made into a sensational beauty," she explained. "I just wanted to be restored." Her surgeon was able to do just that. In two separate operations, he implanted a silicone-filled sac under her skin where the breast had been removed, then reduced the size of the other breast to make it more nearly resemble the new one. The result is not a duplication of Mrs. Dawson's pre-1970 figure, but she is delighted nevertheless. Says she: "I can finally look at myself in the mirror without wincing."

La reconstitution des seins

Une Newyorkaise de 54 ans, Mme Joan Dawson* subit en 1970 l'ablation du sein gauche atteint de cancer et passa les trois années suivantes à lutter contre la dépression et le traumatisme de la mutilation. Un beau jour, elle décide d'agir. La plupart des femmes, en pareil cas, vont s'en remettre à un psychiatre, mais Mme Dawson, elle, retourne chez son médecin pour qu'il lui refasse un sein. "Je ne voulais pas qu'il me transforme en une beauté sensationnelle, a-t-elle expliqué par la suite, mais simplement qu'il élimine les traces de l'amputation." Elle avait frappé à la bonne porte. Le chirurgien inséra sous la peau un sac de silicone en remplacement de la glande mammaire et, par une seconde intervention, il réduisit les proportions de l'autre sein pour le rendre à peu près de la même grosseur que le sein artificiel. Mme Dawson n'a pas retrouvé sa silhouette d'avant 1970, mais elle est enchantée du résultat. " Je peux enfin me regarder dans un miroir sans grimacer," a-t-elle confié.
*Ce nom est fictif.

LEVEL ONE: OBSERVING CONVENTIONS OF FORM

The first level is that of standard writing practices, which encompass all the formal rules of presentation that differ from one language to another: conventional abbreviations—of courtesy titles for example; units of time and measurement; forms of numbers and symbols; use of capital letters in titles, proper names, place names, and historical names; word division; spelling;

and punctuation and other marks.[1] As well, they include the proper etiquette for administrative and business correspondence and other labels, codes, and conventions used in pragmatic texts.

Grammatical rules also come into play at this first level of language manipulation. In theory a student entering a university course in translation is already well versed in grammar; the reality is quite otherwise. Nevertheless, a translation course is not the place for systematic instruction in grammar, for that would sidetrack the course from its real objective. Each student must take responsibility for bringing his knowledge of grammar up to par. It is difficult to imagine anyone being able to study translation without having a firm grasp of spelling, syntax, and punctuation.

In the passage cited above, the French spelling of "Mrs" as "Mme," the differing use of quotation marks around direct speech (in French the short interpolations such as "a-t-elle expliqué" are placed inside the quotation marks, whereas in English they are not), the use of upper case letters in English titles, and grammatical agreements are examples of conventions of form.

This is the level of the "mechanics" of style, which are a matter of knowledge, pure and simple. Differences in French and English usage at this level can easily be taught in a systematic way in an introductory translation course; the comparative method is ideal. However, this level of language manipulation should not be too heavily emphasized, because the real difficulties in translation lie elsewhere.[2] I did not include any exercises on conventions of form in the original French edition of this book, preferring to give more attention to the three other levels of language manipulation, which are of more interest from both the theoretical and pedagogical points of view.

---

1. These rules are set down in codes (spelling, grammatical, typographical). They are arbitrary and conventional, as are linguistic signs, road signs, and the rules of games. Imposed by the demands of life in society, conventions of form are institutionalized and considered obligatory by the speakers of the language to which they apply. By conforming to them, one implicitly affirms one's allegiance to the community and demonstrates the desire to optimize the process of written communication. In that sense, conventions of form fall within the scope of discourse analysis.

2. An error in punctuation can, however, completely alter meaning, as the following anecdote illustrates. A woman found the fur coat of her dreams in a department store. It was extremely expensive, so she sent a telegram to her husband, who was abroad on business, asking if she could buy the coat. Staggered by the outrageous price, her husband immediately wired in the negative: DEFINITELY NOT, TOO EXPENSIVE FOR YOU MY DEAR. Fortunately for his wife, the telegraph operator omitted the punctuation, thus reversing the meaning of the message: DEFINITELY NOT TOO EXPENSIVE FOR YOU MY DEAR. A comma can be very costly.

Accents on capital letters are another example. Sometimes it is necessary to convince non-French speakers to put accents on upper case (and also lower case) letters by pointing out to them that BISCUITS SALES (dirty crackers) are not the same as BISCUITS SALÉS (salted crackers), and that a box of BISCUITS SALES simply would not sell. Accents and punctuation marks can have semantic value.

LEVEL TWO: PERFORMING INTERPRETIVE ANALYSIS

We have seen that interpretation is an interior hermeneutic dialogue between the translator and the source text. This dialogue, which leads to the translator's grasping the meaning of the linguistic signs, ranges over every word and utterance in the text. However, not all parts of the text require the same degree of interpretive analysis to be understood and re-expressed. In fact, some words and grammatical constructions can be rendered in the target text instantly without much intellectual effort on the translator's part. Other words, sentences, or idiomatic expressions, however, demand some reflection. Sometimes it is extremely difficult even to express the meaning in the target language. It is worthwhile to try to ascertain the reasons for such momentary blocks. Lack of language knowledge is not the sole explanation; in fact, it often has nothing to do with the problem. Even experienced translators can be momentarily paralyzed by a group of words or a turn of phrase. Specialized terms in a general text will, of course, slow down the general translator, but it would be a mistake to assume that the difficulty in expressing a term in the target language is necessarily related to either the technical nature of the term or its rarity. In a translation seminar it often happens that whole groups of students are baffled by a passage. Even though the usual significations of the words are known, the meaning cannot be grasped or re-verbalized in the target language. We will see later that the difficulty arises not from the words' intrinsic significations, but from their meaning in context.

Understanding why this occurs is crucial to discourse analysis and translation pedagogy. In attempting to explain the phenomenon, it is helpful to distinguish three different degrees of interpretive analysis:
   a) transfer of monosemous words (no analysis required)
   b) retrieval of standard equivalents from the linguistic system (simple analysis required)
   c) re-creation in context (detailed analysis required)

Transfer of Monosemous Words

The proportion varies, but every text to be translated contains some elements of information that do not require interpretive analysis or reasoning by analogy. These elements can be understood and re-expressed without interpretation. They are monosemous[3] words that the translator can transpose

---

3. "Monosemous" is used here in its usual sense of "having one meaning," and "polysemous" as "having many meanings." "Laryngology," for example, is monosemous, while "foot" is polysemous. The two terms are not used in the technical sense given to them by some linguists (such as Bernard Pottier), who espouse componential analysis or are developing a semantic theory within the framework of transformational grammar. For them a seme is a semantic trait characterizing a concept. "The purpose of semic analysis is to establish the semantic composition of a lexical unit by examining semantic traits, or semes, minimal units of signification that cannot be independently realized." ("L'analyse sémique vise à établir la composition sémantique d'une unité lexicale par la considération de traits sémantiques ou sèmes, unités minimales de signification non susceptibles de réalisation indépendante.") Dubois et al., *Dictionnaire de linguistique*, at entry for "sémique."

directly to the target text without referring to the context or the situation. He can transfer them more or less mechanically from one text to the other. Proper names, numbers, and most scientific terms fall into this category of monosemous words that have a purely symbolic value.

This fact about monosemous words has been demonstrated experimentally. In her study of note-taking by consecutive interpreters, Danica Seleskovitch found that interpreters always write down such words because monosemous terms have to do with knowledge, not comprehension. She explains that "[These] terms are difficult to memorize because they do not lend themselves to the use of reason and do not require any analytical effort."[4] Such terms are, for all intents and purposes, isolated in discourse, having no meaning other than their linguistic signification. The *Time* article cited above contains examples of cases where meaning and signification are identical: "Joan Dawson," "cancer," "1970," "54," "three," "psychiatrist," "surgeon," and "silicone."

"New York City" is another example, but here the translator chose to combine the proper name with another element of information ("of") in order to form a noun that would be the subject of the first sentence: "Une Newyorkaise de 54 ans, Mme Joan Dawson . . ." Such semantic concentration, which entails moving and reorganizing elements of information, is one of the most characteristic features of translation. We will explore this feature more thoroughly when we discuss the fourth level of language manipulation, textual organicity. The fact that "New York City" has here been "enriched" by an additional seme does not alter its monosemous nature.

In summary, with a few exceptions[5] (those traps lying in wait for the translator at every turn), every text contains terms that require no interpretation because they are monosemous. Polysemous words are a completely different matter, as we shall see next.

Retrieval of Standard Equivalents from the Linguistic System

The simplest form of interpretation is practised on words whose meaning can be deduced from the linguistic context and reproduced in the target language using nothing more than knowledge and memory of languages. The translator identifies the relevant signification of the word or syntagma in context, knowing that he will be able to find a word in the target language

---

4. "La difficulté de [leur] mémorisation est due au fait que ces termes ne se prêtent à aucun raisonnement et ne suscitent aucun effort d'analyse." Seleskovitch, *Langage, langues et mémoire*, p. 25.

5. Some examples are units of measurement that must be converted (10 mph becomes 16 km/h); proper names that must be adapted (Mrs Smith translated by Mme Dupont in France or Mme Tremblay in Quebec) because they are used as generic names rather than being proper names in the true sense; eponymous terms that may be different in another language (names of illnesses, scientific laws). Such words require some interpretation because their translation depends on the nature and destination of the text (see next section, "Retrieval of Standard Equivalents from the Linguistic System").

that speakers of that language would normally and naturally use to designate the same reality in the same communication situation.[6] Equivalences of this type are fixed, and many of them appear in bilingual dictionaries or works on comparative stylistics.

Let us take as an example the word "removal" in the first line of "Rebuilding the Breast." In interpreting this word, the translator considers both its broader context (in this case a medical text) and its immediate context, the words on either side of it ("After the removal of her left breast because of cancer . . ."), because even in a medical text, "removal" could have a signification other than the one which is used here: "act of surgically excising a limb, organ, or tumour." When "removal" is used in this sense, the corresponding French word is usually "ablation," which in standard reference works has a signification identical to that of "removal." The two terms match perfectly in what might be called semantic isomorphism. Other examples of words that illustrate the first degree of interpretation are breast: sein, years: années, depression: dépression, she decided: elle décide, most women: la plupart des femmes, situation: cas, her doctor: son médecin, I didn't want to: je ne voulais pas, sensational beauty: beauté sensationnelle, skin: peau, figure: silhouette, finally: enfin.

These examples are valid for *this text only*. There is a difference between saying that "ablation" is the only possible translation of "removal" and saying that in a certain text, the best word for conveying the concept expressed by "removal," taking into account its meaning and immediate context, is "ablation." It would be incorrect to maintain that it will always be possible to retrieve a standard equivalent for "removal" from the linguistic system. That same word could very well necessitate further interpretive analysis in another context (see next section, "Re-Creation in Context"). One can say, however, that it can never be treated as a monosemous word. The purpose of interpretation is to discover the contextual meaning of words, which do not always combine in the same way. *Discourse analysis approaches texts as relative and individual entities. Two statements identical in form are considered different if they occur in different speech situations.* This is one of the postulates of discourse analysis.

Making semantic matches by retrieving accepted equivalents from the linguistic system is not transcoding, for transcoded equivalences are estab-

---

6.   By language is meant not only the potentialities of the code (lexicon and combinatorial rules), but also all the fixed expressions required by usage and therefore belonging as much to language as to discourse. For example, the note "For reference only" on the cover of a reference book in a library summons up in French the fixed expression "À consulter sur place." Both are received expressions belonging to the linguistic resources of English and French, as are the metaphorical expressions "a tempest in a teapot" and "une tempête dans un verre d'eau," or the highway signs "One way" and "Sens unique."

lished without reference to any real communication situation. Here, it is the context that determines the interpretation of "removal" and the translator's recall of the expressive resources of French that subsequently (or simultaneously) enables him to suggest "ablation" as an equivalent.

When forty-four students translated the text "Rebuilding the Breast," thirty used the word "ablation" in the first sentence, eight the verbal locution "se faire enlever," and six the expression "mammectomie du sein gauche." It is not by chance that nearly seventy per cent of the students chose the first solution, though the other two are perfectly acceptable. The explanation lies in the fact that there is an unchanging reality that transcends the text: language as a collective instrument of expression. Such is not always the case, for other words and groups of words can be interpreted in an astonishing variety of ways and give rise to a wide range of solutions, some of them contradictory (see p. 92).

It is this degree of interpretation that most of the excellent examples in *Stylistique comparée du français et de l'anglais* illustrate. Vinay and Darbelnet take stylistics and language[7] as one and the same and show how to translate French into English, and vice versa, by focusing on the lexical and structural differences between the two linguistic systems. The goal of bilingual discourse analysis, on the other hand, is not to learn how to translate one language into another, but how to reproduce the meaning of a text using the expressive resources of another language. From this point of view, translation is a search for equivalent ways of expressing a single intended meaning. Equivalence in difference: therein lies the central problem of translation. Discourse analysis goes beyond studying the forms or structures of language as a system. This will become clearer as I describe re-creation in context and then move on to the third and fourth levels of language manipulation.

Re-Creation in Context

Words and expressions do not always have agreed-upon equivalents in the target language. Consequently, the translator cannot rely on his knowledge of the linguistic system alone to match the idea in the original text with a generally accepted and sanctioned form in the target language. Writers link words together in new ways or give terms meanings that are not found in dictionaries (see "Meaning of Lexical Units," chapter 2). One of the characteristics of natural languages is that, from a finite number of phonemes,

---

7. According to Jean-Paul Vinay, "Works about so-called 'comparative stylistics' usually, if not always, deal with 'universal' language processes." ("Les ouvrages dits de 'stylistique comparée' traitent normalement sinon exclusivement des procédés 'universels' de la langue.") Vinay, "La traduction littéraire," p. 14.

vocables, and structures, an infinite number of utterances can be generated by means of new combinations whose meaning is derived from their context. "Language," according to Danica Seleskovitch, "is a chemistry of meaning and a physics of form. Chemistry, because an infinite number of combinations, each with a new signification, can be created from a limited number of linguistic elements; physics because the elements that combine to give rise to a new signification do not lose their formal identity, as the elements of a chemical compound do."[8] The fact that elements "do not lose their formal identity," while at the same time having an infinity of potential meanings, can make interpretation difficult. Words that take on an unusual meaning in context can be an obstacle to understanding. The idea to be reformulated can also disconcert, or seem suspect to, the translator if it is inconsistent with his own system of moral, social, or aesthetic values. The translator is no more a psychological abstraction than the writer is.

The syntagma "a sense of loss" in the sentence "Mrs Joan Dawson, 54, of New York City, spent the next three years battling depression and a sense of loss," has a meaning particular to that context, even though the expression is common in English and is often used in obituaries—for example, "We all share a deep sense of loss at the passing of America's best-loved artist, Norman Rockwell." (The following comments also apply in principle to the verb "to restore" in the sentence "I didn't want to be made into a sensational beauty . . . I just wanted to be restored.") In this particular English text, the combination of words is used in an idiosyncratic and original way. In order to plumb its meaning, the translator must, drawing on his powers of explication and inference, undertake a more thorough analysis of the context than he would in the case of retrieval of a standard equivalent. Such analysis is all the more necessary when the expression has no "twin" in the other language, no ready-made and agreed-upon equivalent such as the ones that formed the second half of the pairs "removal":"ablation" and "women":"femmes." Knowing the meaning of the individual words "a," "sense," "of" and "loss" is not in itself enough for the translator to produce a semantically equivalent solution; nor can he simply search his linguistic memory for a reformulation of those concepts in the target language. He is faced, not with an untranslatable expression, but with a combination of words that has an unusual, original meaning and therefore demands extra effort in its analysis. Re-creation in context is the only way out of this impasse. No other solution is possible, because the meaning of

---

8.   "Le langage est chimie pour le sens et physique pour les formes. Il est chimie, car il se crée, à partir d'un nombre restreint d'éléments linguistiques, un nombre infini de combinaisons à significations nouvelles; cependant les éléments qui entrent en combinaison pour donner une signification nouvelle ne perdent pas leur identité formelle comme c'est le cas des éléments d'un composé chimique, et la forme du langage est donc, pour l'essentiel, physique." Seleskovitch, *Langage, langues et mémoire*, pp. 49-50.

this particular assemblage of words is a product of the dynamics of language use; it is not given by the language system alone. Just as the lexicon of a language is structured by its semantic networks,[9] the meaning of certain words or groups of words is dependent on the semantic forces generated by the text itself, which exponentially increases the potential of the language.

Because there is no standard equivalent, a contextual, conceptual equivalent must be found. The text is a unified whole, a microsystem of inter-dependent elements. The etymology of *context* can be traced back to "weaving together." It appears that the laws of structuralism hold true at the level of discourse as well as at the level of language.

Viewed from too close, a single brush-stroke in a painting might look awkward, but from a few steps back it blends in perfectly with the rest of the canvas. The same is true of terms or syntagmas that require re-creation in context; they must be analyzed in the light of the text as a whole. In order to infer their semantic and logical relationships with the other terms and to invest them with the appropriate meaning, the translator must step back and detach himself from the purely linguistic signification of the terms.

Any teacher of practical translation courses will have had ample opportunity to observe how much difficulty beginners experience in resolving such thorny problems. Still unsure of the proper approach to adopt toward the original text, there are some who, through an excess of caution, do not dare part from it, and cling to the signs of the source language like hapless survivors to the wreckage of their ship. Thinking that a literal translation is bound to be an accurate one, they fall back on the solution closest in form to the original. They give in to the temptation to transcode, and are likely to translate "a sense of loss" by "un sentiment de perte" or "une sensation de perte." But by sticking to the letter they lose the spirit of the message; transcoded equivalents and contextual equivalents are often irreconcilably at odds.

Other students, sensing intuitively that exaggerated deference to the word will "enervate the meaning" ("énerve le sens"), as Voltaire said, rightly shy away from literal translation. However, many tend to push the interpretation too far, forgetting that the purpose of *detaching* oneself from the form of the original is to *draw closer* to its meaning, not further away from it. The translator's licence is not absolute. His interpretation is limited by the text, which he must interrogate if he is to convert his vague and impressionistic intuitions into a faithful translation.

It is easy to verify that a passage requiring considerable interpretive analysis can engender a wide variety of renditions in the target language.

---

9. "Language is a system of interdependent terms in which the value of each term results solely from the simultaneous presence of the others." Saussure, *Course in General Linguistics*, p. 114 [159]. Structuralism recognizes the predominance of structure, and thus of relations, over unity. It does not define linguistic unity in terms of its intrinsic characteristics alone; instead, it stresses relational characteristics.

The number of different ways in which students interpreted "a sense of loss" is striking; thirteen interpretations were to be found in the forty-four assignments handed in. While some students concentrated on the concept of loss, producing literal and unimaginative translations, others saw disgust, abandonment, frustration, infirmity, or even uselessness. This is a far cry from the consensus underlying the translation of "removal" by "ablation." The seemingly innocuous expression presents a translation difficulty that "removal" did not.[10] The question is: how does the translator go about extracting a likely meaning from the syntagma "a sense of loss"? How does he re-create a concept in context? There is a considerable difference between "un sentiment d'abandon" ("a feeling of abandonment"), "le sentiment d'être perdue" ("the feeling that she was lost"), "le sentiment d'avoir perdu une partie d'elle-même" ("the feeling that she had lost a part of herself"), "un vide des plus profonds qui s'était emparé de tout son être" ("a profound void that had swallowed her soul"), and "elle se sentait diminuée" ("she felt diminished"), all of which were proposed by students given the text to translate.

The comparative method is of no help in solving the double problem of interpretation and reformulation, because no point of comparison is available. It is only by analyzing the lexical network and reasoning logically that one can arrive at an acceptable solution. The process involves observation, intuition, judgement, and intelligence; it is diametrically opposed to mechanical translation, whether by a machine or by an unthinking translator. Let us attempt to follow one possible course of interpretation.

Phase 1—Contextual Analysis
In this text, the words "removal," "breast," "cancer," "operations," and "doctor" clearly situate the reader in a medical context and define a general area for conceptual and lexical investigation. The immediate context ("[She spent] three years battling *depression*. . . . Most women in the same situation turn to a *psychiatrist*") refers more specifically to the particular branch of medicine that is concerned with emotional problems, the pathologies of the psyche. In that light, "a sense of loss" evokes "an emotional blow" caused by "the loss of a breast." It appears that this emotional blow is at the root of the "depression" that Mrs Dawson is "battling."

Phase 2—Conceptual Analysis
In French, psychoanalysts refer to a condition of mental or emotional shock as "traumatisme" ("trauma"). Surgeons have at least six words in French for the act of removing a diseased part of the body: "ablation," "amputa-

---

10.   For further discussion of the notion of difficulty, see p. 94.

tion," "excision," "exérèse," "résection," and "mutilation." This last term, unlike the five others, has a negative connotation of degradation; speaking figuratively, one could say for example that a famous painting or a text had been mutilated ("la mutilation d'un tableau célèbre"; "la mutilation d'un texte"). The other words do not have the same connotation; they are more neutral, strictly medical terms, with the exception of "amputation," which can, in its figurative sense, refer to a loss or removal ("La pièce a été amputée de trois scènes") without necessarily having a pejorative connotation. Surely it is because Mrs Dawson felt mutilated that she slid into a depression. She would not have experienced so violent a reaction had she undergone an appendectomy or a tonsillectomy. This is the reasoning that led me to select the expression "le traumatisme de la mutilation" as a contextual equivalent of "a sense of loss," though it is by no means the only possible solution. A different line of reasoning could easily have been pursued.

The students translating the text reproduced most of the major semantic elements of the English syntagma—the ideas of "loss," of "degradation," of "emotional blow," of "inner void"—in their assignments. These concepts served as starting points for contextual reasoning.

This brief analysis of the process by which concepts are re-created in context clearly shows that it is neither through inspiration nor through vague subjective impressions that meaning is elucidated, but through a rigorous analysis—one that does not, however, exclude intuition. *Interlinguistic comparison does not enter into the attempt to discover meaning.* The interpretive process is in this case the only valid method. The text normally contains enough clues for the translator to summon the knowledge he needs to arrive at a functional equivalent (which here is the psychological after-effects of major surgery).

From the point of view of interpretation alone, the difference between retrieving standard equivalents from the linguistic system (as with "removal") and re-creating concepts in context (as with "a sense of loss") is similar to the difference, in algebra, between an equation with one unknown and an equation with two unknowns. An equation is a formal statement of equality or equivalence between mathematical or logical expressions. The search for a translation equivalent is also an attempt at equality, since its goal is to give the same semantic weight to two words, two expressions, or two utterances. In both cases, establishing the relationship is conditional upon the values attributed to the two unknowns.

In the case of retrieval, the meaning of the original expression does not pose any particular problems of interpretation; the only unknown is the existing equivalent in the target language designating the same concept in the same speech situation. To re-create a concept in context, the translator must attribute values to two unknowns: first he must establish the meaning of the expression in its original context, then he must explore the possibilities of the target language in order to construct an expression that semantically and stylistically balances the first one. Bilingual discourse analysis enables us to appreciate the creative aspect of interlinguistic transfer. Indeed, some aspects of language will always be hidden from those who study only a *single* language.

Are expressions that entail re-creation of a concept in context more difficult to translate than those that simply involve the retrieval of a word from the other linguistic system? This question raises a second one: by what criteria should the difficulty of a text be assessed? Difficulty of translation does not lend itself to definition, primarily because it is relative and subjective. In fact, it can only be gauged *statistically*, in terms of the *number of pitfalls the text contains for a given group of individuals*. Beginners will stumble where an experienced translator proceeds smoothly, having learned over the years how to circumvent obstacles. A skill—and translation is a skill—develops with practice. A translator who has mastered his craft will know how to avoid traps and overcome obstacles. The teacher must, therefore, evaluate his students' performance accurately if he is to tailor his methodology to their specific needs.

Instead of dogmatically and arbitrarily declaring that a given aspect of the manipulation of language was bound to be a stumbling block for beginning translators, I chose to take an empirical approach and sought to determine why certain passages of a text were almost always well translated, while others were less often rendered satisfactorily in the target language. In the course of correcting the translations of some fifty university students, I observed that certain types of errors recurred. Compiling, analyzing, and classifying these errors led me to conclude that there were three different degrees of interpretive analysis.

Statistical data confirmed that a high proportion of beginning students had more difficulty in re-expressing a passage that required interpretation and re-creation of a concept than in retrieving standard equivalents. In four groups of students the results were as follows:

Transfer of monosemous terms—99 per cent correct solutions
Retrieval of standard equivalents—70 per cent correct solutions
Re-creation in context—less than 50 per cent correct solutions

The high percentage of correct solutions in the transfer of monosemous terms is due to the fact that the errors are mainly careless, such as the incorrect transcription of a date or number, or the omission of a monosemous word in the target text. Errors in retrieval of standard equivalents indicate a lack of knowledge of the resources of the target language. Errors in re-creation in context reveal as well that a segment of the original text has been at least partly misunderstood. It should be noted that inevitably some subjectivity is involved in judging whether the solutions are faithful to the meaning of the original message. This can be demonstrated simply by asking several different markers to evaluate the fidelity of the translations in students' papers for "a sense of loss" and "to be restored." It is safe to say that not every marker would rate the same solutions as acceptable equivalents. The total of correct solutions would, however, hover around fifty per cent.

It might be objected that translating a monosemous word such as a little-known scientific term is equally difficult as translating a combination of words such as "a sense of loss" or "I just wanted to be restored." However, it must be pointed out that the problem here is not one of interpretation, but one of knowledge of language. Often it is a translator's scanty knowledge of scientific vocabulary—an understandable shortcoming—that hinders him from re-expressing scientific realities in the target language. Scientific terms and the phenomena they designate are objects of knowledge, not of interpretation. Therefore, when a terminological problem such as this is encountered, the translator turns to specialized dictionaries, which refresh his memory and point him in the right direction as he reformulates the text. Re-expressing concepts in a second language requires both knowledge and the ability to interpret. If the cognitive processes involved in translation are to be properly understood, the interpretation of discourse must not be confounded with the general and linguistic knowledge on which that interpretation is based.

Difficulty of translation is thus a purely statistical notion, being a function of both the idiosyncrasies of the text and the abilities of the translator. It is impossible to state a priori that one text is inherently easier or harder to translate than another. The only way difficulty can be assessed, and then only roughly, is through statistical analysis of the types of errors made by groups of translation students. The analysis would, however, benefit from the use of the three different degrees of interpretive analysis for establishing grading systems and rating difficulty of translation, neither of which translation pedagogy has yet done. Work such as this would perhaps enable us to clearly separate mistakes resulting from poor command of the technique itself from mistakes due to ignorance of languages and life, even though the line separating the two is admittedly blurred.

The three different degrees of interpretive analysis, then, are decidely not translation "procedures," as that word is used in *Stylistique comparée*. Nor are they recipes for semantic transfer. A translator may turn out good work without ever having heard of this hierarchy of interpretation of linguistic signs. The scheme of three different degrees of interpretation does, however, clarify the internal dynamics of discourse by showing that lexical items do not all undergo the same analysis as the translator determines the meaning of a passage. It is also very useful in translation pedagogy because it makes the cognitive processes underlying translation easier to understand, and helps explain the recurrent types of errors made by inexperienced translators. When experience—in this case careful analysis of performance—is taken as the point of departure in the construction of a theory, it is then easy to descend from the theoretical realm to the realities of language and find pedagogical applications for the principles inferred from observation. A theory grounded in practice has a firm foundation; similarly, a pedagogy with solid theoretical underpinnings derived from experience is likely to have practical value. An example of the pedagogical applications of the three degrees of interpretive analysis can be found in the pedagogical objectives I developed for translation from English to French (Appendix 3). Similar objectives and exercises can be devised for translation between any two languages.

LEVEL THREE: INTERPRETING STYLE

Style is *how* something is written. It consists of everything over and above the purely denotative function of a text, everything added to the bare, unvarnished information. This connotative addition is not, however, without meaning. Content and form, like the two sides of a coin, cannot be separated; they both contribute to the overall meaning of a message and the cognitive and affective impact on the reader. As Riffaterre said, "The message expresses; the style stresses."[11] Even a technical text, which is neutral in tone, can immediately be identified by its terminology as belonging to a well-defined category of writing. The technical, administrative, advertising, legal, and journalistic styles are all characterized by easily identifiable traits, and can be systematically taught in a translation course. It should be noted that it is not specialized terminology alone that characterizes these styles, for neither advertising nor journalism has a distinctive vocabulary.

For the purposes of translation teaching, it is helpful to look at style from a very general point of view and consider it a *functional specialization* of language, without, however, excluding from this definition the appeal to the emotions and the "ornaments" that one immediately associates with the word "style." This pragmatic and general definition of style is similar to the notion of form stripped of any reference to art or originality. In very general terms, then, the style of a pragmatic text is basically equivalent to its form. The translator respects the form by adhering to all the rules governing codified languages, by rendering the affective aspects in certain types of texts, or both. An insurance policy or a collective agreement is not written in the same way as a tourist brochure, an advertisement, or an administrative report.

There are four elements involved in any text: the author, the subject, the vector (genre of text, type of language used), and the intended audience. In its broadest sense, style is simply respect for the constraints imposed by

---

11. "Le message exprime, [tandis que] le style souligne."

these four elements. Style is part and parcel of communication. The translator of pragmatic texts, therefore, must comply with certain stylistic requirements to communicate effectively.

What are the four elements in the text "Rebuilding the Breast"? The article is not signed, so we do not know who the author is, but that is of no consequence in pragmatic texts (see p. 10). The subject is a popularized description of a new breast reconstruction technique. The vector is a news article, containing simple medical terminology, whose purpose is to convey information. The intended audience is the millions of readers of *Time* magazine. The translator must therefore respect not only the lexical and structural constraints imposed by the target language, but also the journalistic style of the article, which here is not particularly marked, and its medical tone.

Defining the style of news articles is not easy because their subject matter is so wide-ranging. As a general rule, however, journalists focus on the most spectacular or unusual aspect of any fact or event, occasionally even going too far. Indeed, they have a reputation for dealing in sensationalism. The fondness for the unusual is evident in the style or form of their articles, particularly in the opening paragraphs. For example:

The Grueling Baby Chase

Sweat. Nakedness. Intimacy. Union. Fertilization *in vivo*. Once upon a time, all babies were conceived that way—and when it didn't work, a husband and wife had just one choice to make: living without offspring or adopting a child. More recently drugs and surgery have allowed many couples to triumph over infertility— but they still had to make love to make babies. Then, in 1978, Aldous Huxley's 1932 science-fiction vision of "test tube" babies became reality with the birth of Louise Brown, conceived when her parents' egg and sperm were joined in a glass dish (*In vitro*). So radical was this new technology that it suddenly seemed possible that infertility might be largely eradicated, like polio or smallpox. Unfortunately, the brave new world of IVF (in vitro fertilization) hasn't worked out that way. (*Newsweek*, Nov. 30, 1987)

Life among the Sexually Deviant: Area Psychiatrist Patron Saint of the Perverted

John Bradford left a world of discrimination in South Africa. John Bradford fights a world of discrimination in Canada.

He fights so tirelessly that his wife Jill says she's glad they've completed their family. "I say that because we don't go to bed together and we don't wake up together." (*Ottawa Citizen*, Dec. 26, 1987)

New Rx: Try an Atemoya a Day

Plant avocados, everyone urged Marc Ellenby. It was 1980, and Ellenby had just purchased eight and a half acres in subtropical Dade County, Fla.—prime land for what was then a thriving avocado industry. But it wasn't avocados that had lured Ellenby from the Midwest to Florida. Instead he took a chance with sweetsop, or sugar apples, a fruit beloved in much of the world but not a commercial crop here until Ellenby and his wife, Kiki, harvested their first 4,000 pounds in 1982. Today the Florida avocado industry is flat; and the Ellenbys, working some 70 acres, run one of the largest independent tropical-fruit businesses in the state. (*Newsweek*, Nov. 23, 1987)

These examples show that journalists communicate facts ("the message expresses") while at the same time emphasizing as much as possible ("the style stresses") whatever is most likely to capture the reader's attention, particularly in the opening paragraphs. In the article on rebuilding the breast, the author seeks to capture the reader's interest by describing the actual experience of a woman who has had her breast removed and emphasizing the originality of her approach to easing the subsequent emotional pain. The woman is given a pseudonym in order to protect her identity while at the same time giving the reader someone to identify with, thus adding dramatic intensity to the story. In the taut style characteristic of *Time* magazine, Mrs Dawson's determination is expressed in three short, juxtaposed sentences:

> Then she decided to do something about it. Most women in the same situation turn to a psychiatrist. Mrs Dawson (not her real name) went to her doctor and asked him to rebuild her missing breast.

Rather than simply transposing this juxtaposition, it seems preferable, in crossing over to the other language, to change the register somewhat, while preserving the original intent. A measure of intuition and subjectivity inevitably enters into this type of stylistic adaptation, although any reliance on these faculties is much disparaged by the proponents of a coldly scientific approach to the study of translation. Translators do not all have the same linguistic sensibility, and opinions often differ as to the best way of conveying the spirit of a message. Their perceptions of the communicative aspect of a text vary.[12] I have already argued that the translation of pragmatic texts is an *art* of re-expression; this is true not only of the substance of texts but also of their style.

The resources of the French language are rich enough to provide the translator with a wide range of stylistic options, from which he can choose the most *functional* affective and communicative elements possible for the message in the target language:

> *Un beau jour*, elle dé*ci*de d'agir. La plupart des femmes, en pareil cas, vont s'en remettre à un psychiatre, *mais* Mme Dawson, *elle*, retour*ne* chez son médecin pour qu'il lui refasse un sein.

---

12. On the distinction between "communicative translation" and "semantic translation," see Newmark's "Communicative and Semantic Translation."

Three techniques help render the spirit of the text: the use of the historical present tense ("décide"; "retourne"), the addition of certain words for emphasis ("un beau jour"; "elle"), and the use of a conjunction ("mais") to connect the third and fourth clauses of the second sentence. Of course, these are not the only options available. They are, however, one means of achieving the double goal of bringing out the originality of the woman's decision and arousing the reader's curiosity, thus compelling him to read on.

To give the article a medical tone, the translator draws on specialized vocabulary and medical phraseology. "Subir l'ablation d'un sein" is more of a medical expression than "se faire enlever un sein" or "l'enlèvement d'un sein"; the same can be said of "atteint de cancer," compared with "à cause de cancer." The term "dépression" ("depression") denotes a pathological state, which is a medical phenomenon, and cannot be replaced by words such as "désespoir" ("despair") or "cafard" ("blues"), even though their meaning may be close to that of "dépression" or included in it.

The medical nature of the article makes it possible to vary the translation of "breast" by using "glande mammaire" instead of "sein." "Glande mammaire" would probably not be an acceptable synonym for "sein" in a poem, given its obviously anatomical reference—though one can never be too sure, since poetry is an attempt to break through the barriers of language. (Much remains to be said about synonymy in discourse, which is one of the concerns of discourse analysis. Synonymy does not follow the same rules in context as it does in language; contextual and language synonymy are opposed just as contextual and transcoded equivalence are. This is a fruitful area for investigation.) It is also the medical nature of the text that justifies the translation of "the new one" by "sein artificiel" (modelled on "bras artificiel" and "jambe artificielle") and of "to be restored" by "éliminer les traces de l'amputation." Indeed, the very title of the article, "La reconstitution des seins," has a medical ring to it. One of the senses of "reconstitution" is the biological regeneration of injured tissues or organs. In the case described here, a breast is mechanically rebuilt using a silicone prosthesis; by analogy with biological regeneration, the term "reconstitution" is used here to describe the process by which something is restored to its normal state or form.

I do not wish to claim that the translation I have proposed here is a perfect model of form. The purpose of these reflections on style is to establish the principle that, in the case of pragmatic texts, the choice of a style is as much a matter of the subject of the text, the function of the message, and the intended audience, as of the vector itself.

The following example shows how the nature and function of a text can influence linguistic choices. It is taken from a car manufacturer's promotional brochure: "The company offers an engine guarantee of 5 years or 60,000 miles, whichever comes first." From a strictly semantic point of view, a French translation such as this one would be quite acceptable: "La garantie-moteur de la compagnie expire au bout de 5 ans ou dès que la voiture atteint 60 000 milles." Although the grammar, words, syntax, and meaning are all correct, this formulation does not make sense from a business point of view. The nature and destination of the message compel the translator to reject this solution and find a different way of communicating the same ideas. One of the golden rules of advertising is that it is always preferable to state something in positive terms rather than negative. Instead of saying that "Pasta won't make you fat," it is better to say—even if it is stretching the truth a little—that "Pasta keeps you slim." Similarly, the warranty can hardly be said to "run out" or "expire," because both expressions have a negative connotation in this communicative situation. It is better to put the message in a positive light, emphasizing the company's generosity and commitment. The translator could say "honorer une garantie," or stress how long the warranty lasted.

Here are a few possible ways of rendering the exclusive disjunction ("5 years or 60,000 miles") in the advertisement:

—Une garantie de 5 ans/60 000 milles couvre le moteur.[13]

—La compagnie honorera une garantie de 5 ans/60 000 milles sur le moteur.

—Une garantie de 5 ans/60 000 milles vous protège contre toute défectuosité du moteur.

These solutions are acceptable translations of an advertisement. If the disjunction were contained in a legal text, that would be an altogether different matter. To avoid ambiguity, the translator would have to specify that the buyer was not simply being presented with a choice (5 years *or* 60,000 miles) but with a restrictive, or exclusive, alternative such that the realization of one condition automatically precludes the other.

This brief example once again underscores the importance of the functional aspect of texts. A message is not an abstraction, so semantically accurate translations are not always appropriate from a rhetorical point of view. This is another postulate of discourse analysis.

The first level of language manipulation is respect for conventions of form. The second is interpretation and reformulation of the lexical elements of the message. The third—interpretation of style—is superimposed on the second. Style is like a uniform, imposed by the demands of communication, in which the translator clothes his text in order to make it comply with the rules of the genre or touch his readers' emotions.

---

13.   The Renault car-manufacturing company offered a two year/40,000 km "Garantie-plus": "La 'GARANTIE-PLUS' Renault vous protège (pièces et main-d'oeuvre) contre toute défectuosité des pièces ou vice de fabrication du moteur et de la boîte de vitesse. Cette protection vient s'ajouter à la garantie de 12 mois/20 000 km qui couvre toute la voiture selon les limites spécifiées par le constructeur" (from the company's advertising).

Yet even here, there is a limit that the translator must not overstep. As regards style in the very broad sense defined earlier, a new trend is emerging in Canadian translation. Conscious of the very real danger that any language will atrophy if it more often expresses thoughts second-hand than in their original form, as is the case with Canadian French,[14] some translators and revisers have sought to counteract the resulting impoverishment of the language by advocating a form of elegant rewriting of certain pragmatic texts.

Their intentions are certainly honourable, but I fear that this practice might open the way for a modern version of the "belles infidèles." Translation must, by nature, follow the general thought pattern of the original text. It cannot very well take the form of a "variation on a familiar theme" or of an "imitation." Such exercises are in fact free adaptations by another name. Whether adaptation is an effective antidote to a massive dose of translation is another question which, unfortunately, is beyond the scope of this work. It is a matter for another discipline, which I suggest should be called "sociotranslation," after "sociolinguistics."[15] In fact, a good translation possesses all the same qualities as a good adaptation, while a bad adaptation is little better than a bad translation. However, it is possible to put a little colour into an anemic translation without drifting into free adaptation.

One must ask whether a text such as the following could be considered true to the spirit and meaning of "Rebuilding the Breast":

Non, ce n'était plus tenable. Mᵐᵉ Dagenais, Montréalaise de 54 ans, ne pouvait plus supporter l'état dépressif qui l'accablait depuis trois ans. L'ablation d'un sein l'avait profondément affectée. Son moral était au plus bas. Consulter un psychiatre? C'est ce qu'aurait fait toute autre femme, mais pas Mᵐᵉ Dagenais; elle préféra retourner chez le médecin qui l'avait opérée dans l'espoir qu'il puisse faire quelque chose. Elle ne souhaitait pas être transformée en Brigitte Bardot. Son seul désir était de redevenir une femme normalement constituée.

Can such an adaptation be considered translation? The translator does not have licence to do anything he likes with a text. As discussed earlier, he must confine his lexical interpretation to what is reasonable; he must also put limits on his stylistic interpretation so that he does not distort the original

---

14. One wit has said: "In Quebec, English is just French that hasn't been translated yet" ("Au Québec, l'anglais c'est du français encore non traduit").
15. The task of "sociotranslation" would be to study the role played by translation in every aspect of a society, particularly in so-called bilingual and bicultural societies such as Canada. Translation could be a gauge of the relationships between two linguistic communities experiencing acculturation on a daily basis. On this subject, see Poisson, "La traduction, facteur d'acculturation"; Cardinal, "Regard critique sur la traduction"; and Delisle, "Projet d'histoire de la traduction."

text by using a style that is out of keeping with it. *The art of translation is the art of hewing to the golden mean. Learning to stay within the limits of fidelity to the author's intention is the hardest lesson to learn, and the truest test of a translator's maturity.* The translator must say neither too little nor too much; this is one of the basic rules of the discipline. The ideal of fidelity is all the more difficult to achieve because sometimes it is necessary to move away from the original formulation in order to be faithful to the meaning, whereas at other times it is necessary to follow the original formulation in order to choose the proper phrasing in the target text. One of the teacher's tasks is to guide the inexperienced translator in making choices, including stylistic choices.

LEVEL FOUR: PRESERVING TEXTUAL ORGANICITY

A text develops according to an internal logic that gives it coherence. The logic is analogous to the invisible framework of beams and girders supporting a building. In a translation, the sentences must be organized so as to follow the development of the thought in the original text. If a text is likened to a building, what I call "textual organicity" is the framework, and style is the external appearance. Organicity is an inherent quality of texts, distinct from idiomaticity. Idiomaticity, as opposed to grammaticality, refers to compliance with the characteristic mode of expression of a language, or the genius of a language, whereas organicity refers to the hierarchical interdependence of all the elements of a text. The organic level is that of the general dynamics of a passage. A text is analyzed from the idiomatic point of view for its adherence to norms; it is studied from the organic point of view for its structure.

In more concrete terms, textual organicity has to do with the links between sentences, the clarity of relationships between elements of information, and the intent underlying the development of ideas or emotions (and not the ideas or emotions themselves) in the various types of writing (such as argumentative, descriptive, narrative, and factual). A reviser describes a translator who is able to write cohesive texts as having a "feeling for the language," or producing translations that "flow well." By that he means that the translator has the ability either to connect ideas explicitly using transitional devices or to link them implicitly. It simply is not enough to correctly translate each word, sentence, or stylistic effect in a text, for the message must form an organic, living whole.

Novice translators need to be taught that written language requires more coherence than spoken language does (see p. 11). Because their attention is focused on solving lexical and syntactical problems, they neglect to keep in mind a view of the text as a whole. This rather natural tendency to translate words or sentences no doubt explains the disjointed nature of some translations. They seem to have been translated sentence by detached sentence; they are jerky, spasmodic. The flow of ideas suffers from interruptions, and the logical relationships are not made clear. Sometimes the relationships established are wrong. A common error in French is to use as the subject of a sentence a pronoun whose antecedent is not the subject of the previous sentence. A careless error of this sort is indicative of carelessly organized ideas. More serious errors are apparent in this passage from a student's translation:

> Atteinte de cancer, une dame de New York âgée de 54 ans, Mme Joan Dawson, s'est fait enlever le sein gauche en 1970. Les trois années qui ont suivi, elle les a passées à combattre la dépression et le sentiment de perte. À la fin, elle a décidé de faire quelque chose pour remédier à la situation.

Although this version conveys most of the meaning of the original, it lacks coherence. "Then" is badly translated by "à la fin," which provides a very awkward transition between the two sentences. The first sentence can easily be made more concise by simplifying "une dame de New York âgée de 54 ans" to "une Newyorkaise de 54 ans" and by placing "atteinte de cancer" after "sein."

Here is another example of a disconnected style in a French translation. The original English read:

> The term cashless society was introduced during the 1960s when we were being told that the wired city would bring the wonders of modern technology into North American lives and homes, revolutionizing our way of living. We were not impressed. We tended to feel that there were other priorities, and environmentalists and social planners showed us the real price of progress. An outstanding feature of the 1970s is the emphasis on human values such as consumers' rights, and the rights of the citizen to privacy.

One student produced the following disjointed translation:

> Durant les années 60, l'idée de la société sans numéraire a fait son apparition. À cette même époque où la citée câblée devait rendre à la portée des habitants de l'Amérique du Nord les merveilles de la technologie moderne, allant même jusqu'à en révolutionner le niveau de vie. Cela n'a suscité guère d'intérêt, puisqu'il semblait y avoir des points beaucoup plus dominants. D'ailleurs les écologistes et les planificateurs sociaux ont fait connaître le vrai prix du progrès. Les années 70 se caractérisent par l'accent porté aux valeurs humaines telles la protection des consommateurs et le respect de la vie privée.

Like the previous example, this translation suffers from lack of coherence. The ideas are developed abruptly, by fits and starts, and the sentences do not flow smoothly. In a coherent text each sentence grows naturally out of the preceding one and leads just as naturally to the sentence that follows. When the logical flow of a text is interrupted time and again, even slightly, the reader eventually becomes annoyed, for he must himself determine how the thoughts are related to each other and must furnish the transitions that the hasty or careless translator did not. The best translation is one that reads least like a translation or a bad piece of prose.

The textual organicity of a translation is a reflection of the translator's ability to think logically and communicate intelligibly. Whatever is worth translating is worth translating clearly. But what exactly is clarity? "Clarity is the courtesy of author to reader," said Jules Renard;[16] this applies equally to the translator. Clarity certainly does not require that only very simple sentences and familiar words be used, to spare the reader intellectual effort. Unfamiliar terms may be used, if they are apposite, as may complex sentences, if they enable the writer to express the subtlety of his thought. In essence, clarity means precise relationships between ideas. Reorganizing concepts to follow the thrust of the original text demands a thorough mastery of language manipulation and great intellectual agility. The translator's skill in executing these mental gymnastics is the measure of his ability to reformulate a message. The logical order of ideas is not necessarily a straight line; it is dictated by the development of the text. The translator must choose syntactic structures according to the internal dynamics of the target text, rather than copying the syntax of the original text (though it often happens that the two syntaxes are similar).

The fourth level of language manipulation, then, is that of the structural changes necessitated by the dynamics of a message. The countless changes made to a text, some required, some optional, stimulate the translator's thought and reveal his abilities as a writer. The changes made to preserve the textual organicity of a text must not, however, be confused with those imposed by the constraints of the target language. "After the removal of *her* left breast," for example, cannot be translated as "Après l'ablation de *son* sein gauche" because in French the personal possessive adjective is not normally used with parts of the body. In French one says, "J'ai mal à *la* tête" or "Elle s'est coupé *un/le* doigt." The structural change "subit en 1970 l'ablation *du* sein gauche" is therefore obligatory because of the nature of the French language. Changes made for the sake of textual organicity are of a different order altogether; they are engendered by the internal movement of the text and may take various forms, as the following examples show.

Redistribution of elements of information
If the meaning of the original text is to be transmitted accurately, "1970" cannot be positioned after the syntagma "atteint de cancer" as in the English

---

16. "La clarté est la politesse des auteurs."

"After the removal of her left breast because of cancer in 1970," because the literal translation "atteint de cancer en 1970" distorts the meaning of the original by making it seem that the cancer, not the removal, occurred in 1970. The translator avoided this error simply by juxtaposing the verb and the date and wrote "subit en 1970 l'ablation du scin gauche atteint de cancer." For the sake of clarity the translator also preferred not to use the pronoun "he" ("he implanted a silicone-filled sac") but rather its antecedent "surgeon," because in his translation the sentence "Elle avait frappé à la bonne porte" had interrupted the grammatical and logical flow.

Concentration
Signifieds can be concentrated in fewer signifiers than in the original. For example, "Mrs Joan Dawson . . . *of* New York *City* . . ." becomes "Une Newyorkaise . . . Mme Joan Dawson. . . ."

Implicitation or Explicitation
Implicitation, or relying on the context to "translate" certain elements of information, is a way of avoiding faulty verbal equivalents (transcoding). For example:

> a silicone-*filled* sac—un sac de silicone
> Mrs Dawson went to her doctor and *asked him* to rebuild her *missing* breast.—
> Mme Dawson, elle, retourne chez son médecin *pour qu'il lui refasse un sein.*

It should not be thought that a concept has been left untranslated because it does not appear in the target text in the form of a signifier. In this example "asked" and "missing" are translated by the context. Entropy[17] comes into play at the level of the text, not of the sentence. The text is an entity much richer in meaning than the sentence, and one always translates texts, not sentences. It follows that entropy is a concern of discourse analysis, not of sentence linguistics.

---

17.   The term "entropy," designating a loss, was borrowed from thermodynamics and applied to cybernetics. It has also been adopted by some translation theorists (notably Eugene A. Nida, Georges Mounin, and Jean-Paul Vinay). In thermodynamics, the term refers to a degradation of energy into heat, while in cybernetics it refers to the deterioration of a message because of background noise during transmission. In translation, "entropy" would, by analogy, refer to a loss of information resulting from the transfer of certain messages from one language to another. However, entropy is not inherent in the translation process itself. It arises out of the nature of the message to be translated and the process of communication. It only occurs under certain circumstances, which would be interesting to analyze. To assume that the translation process inevitably leads to a degradation is to confuse "pragmatic communication" with "integral communication." Once again, it is important to focus the debate about translation on specific issues: while it is fairly easy to predict that there will be entropy in the translation of a poem, there is no evidence that the translation of a set of operating instructions will be equally vulnerable to entropy, if indeed it is at all.

The translation of "she explained" by "a-t-elle expliqué *par la suite*" is an example of explicitation. Since the quotation is in the past tense ("I didn't want to . . . I just wanted to . . ."), Mrs Dawson's comment was presumably made after the operation took place. It was likely addressed to the author of the article, although the text does not actually indicate this. In any case, the translator thought it worthwhile to add "par la suite," dissociating Mrs Dawson's statement from the preceding sentence in order to make it clear that the conversation had not taken place in the doctor's office. This addition was purely optional.

Use of transitions to link utterances
A good example of a transitional expression is "Un beau jour" for the conjunction "then." This contextual equivalence is made possible by the dynamics of the text. (Note how wide the gap between a transcoded equivalent and a contextual equivalent can be.)

The list of required and optional transformations stemming from the internal development of a message could be extended indefinitely. A text is a logic unto itself, just as a language is a system of classification. Consequently, the ability to identify the key ideas in a text[18] and the dexterity to manipulate concepts and connect them by means of logical links are without a doubt the paramount qualities of a good translator. It is here that the expression "manipulating language" acquires real meaning. Boileau's advice to young writers—"Before you attempt to write, learn to think"[19]—could just as well have been addressed to novice translators.

For a translator, learning to think means developing one's sense of the organic structure of a text and acquiring the skill to tighten up the links between ideas and incorporate sentences into an uninterrupted flow of discourse. A text has a certain life, for it expresses the personality of its author. All texts, to varying degrees, have emotional, intellectual, and imaginative dimensions. To reproduce texts faithfully in another language, it is essential to grasp both their spirit and their cadence.

CONCLUSION

The four levels of language manipulation describe that phase of the translation process in which equivalences are developed—the phase between the starting point and the end point of semantic transfer. They are not labels for the

---

18. Exercises in textual analysis to identify the primary and secondary themes of a text—its internal framework—develop a skill that is directly related to translation. This type of exercise should be a part of any writing course for translators. See Ghenet-Hottois, "Contribution à une méthodologie de la composition."
19. "Avant donc que d'écrire apprenez à penser." Boileau, "L'art poétique," Chant I, v. 150.

transformations that can be observed once the process has been completed. The order in which they are presented here does not reflect successive stages in the cognitive process. We saw earlier that the train of conscious and subconscious thought is difficult to follow; a stylistic effect can be perceived either before or after the semantic and syntactic relationships are grasped.

This brief description of the four levels of language manipulation gives rise to the following observations: (1) the interpretive method is the only means of postulating contextual equivalences; (2) translating is an act of judgement and co-ordination that consists in reconciling the semantic and stylistic imperatives of a discourse while respecting the rules of writing and the requirements of textual organicity; and (3) the translator must possess all the qualities of a good writer.

Translation, indeed, presents all of the difficulties that composition does; in "re-composing" the text in another language, the translator is subject to the same constraints as the writer. What distinguishes translation is that the practitioner of this art of re-expression must assimilate an intention that is not his own, and fashion in another language a written message that is not his own. It is not because they lack intelligence, but because they have not yet learned to resist the hypnotic attraction of the forms of the original that some novices will translate "I just wanted to be restored" as "Je voulais simplement restaurer ma féminité." One of the principal objectives of practical training in translation is to root out all forms of excessive literalism at all four levels of language manipulation.

It is easier to understand at this point why some bilingual persons make poor translators: the aptitudes required to co-ordinate four different levels of language manipulation are not exactly the same as those required to speak a second language. The difficulties that some bilinguals experience in translating are proof that translation cannot be reduced to a strictly linguistic operation. As Peter Newmark has said, "All translation remains a craft requiring a trained skill, continually renewed linguistic and non-linguistic knowledge and a deal of flair and imagination, as well as intelligence and above all common sense."[20]

---

20. Newmark, "Communicative and Semantic Translation," p. 177.

Conclusion

The introductory course in the translation of pragmatic texts proposed in this book represents an attempt to devise a teaching method that puts practical translation exercises in perspective. Translators work on an infinite variety of texts, from simple maintenance instructions to works of poetry, including legal, biblical, official, and technical texts. Faced with the impossibility of designing a single method of instruction equally suited to all types of translation, I chose instead to define specific objectives for training beginners in the rudiments of the art.

However, restricting the course material to pragmatic texts formulated according to the rules of written language was not enough in itself. The method also had to take into account the nature of the translator's bilingualism and, more importantly still, focus on the specific characteristics of translation from one particular language to another—here, from English to French. This required investigating current theories of translation and analyzing the process by which contextual equivalents are postulated.

It then became apparent that translation was an intellectual activity located at the junction of thought, language, and reality. An examination of this heuristic process revealed that translating requires skills in four broad areas: language, general knowledge, comprehension, and re-expression. Discourse analysis of texts and translations showed that linguistic skills alone are inadequate to the task of finding contextual equivalents and, therefore, theoretical models based exclusively on the categories of general or descriptive linguistics cannot provide a satisfactory explanation of an activity as dynamic and complex as translation.

Indeed, the translator must combine linguistic skill with encyclopedic knowledge of the realities comprising the physical and mental universe. One can only translate well what one knows well, and extra-linguistic knowledge is essential to understanding and reformulating a message.

It is his ability to comprehend that enables the translator to extract information from a text, to determine the meaning the original author intended to convey. The translator must be able to comprehend both language and facts. A text embodies thought, and must therefore be interpreted—that is, it must be understood—before it can be re-expressed in another language. Interpretation is a hermeneutic exercise performed by the intelligent mind on the four parameters of written communication: the author, the subject, the function, and the intended audience of a text. Comprehension can be defined as the ability to construct a synthesis of all four parameters. Revisers often criticize beginning translators for having "interpreted" a text rather than simply translating it. This is a poor choice of words, for in fact it is impossible to translate without interpreting meaning. Novice translators err, not in interpreting the text, but in *mis*interpreting it, imputing intentions to the author or rendering his thoughts incorrectly.

However, the good translator not only possesses linguistic and encyclopedic knowledge and the capacity to grasp the meaning of a text, he must also have the ability to re-express it. It is obvious that reformulating a text requires an aptitude for writing. Given the importance of this aspect of translation, it seemed best, for training purposes, to consider the translation of pragmatic texts as an art of re-expression based on writing techniques. Unlike the writer, the translator does not draw on his creative powers to communicate his subjective vision of the world in a work of literature. The translator's creativity lies in his acute sensitivity to the intended meaning of an author and his adroit ability to re-express that intention in another text. He has some freedom in the linguistic means he chooses for accomplishing this re-expression. *Translation is a skill (of interpretation and re-expression) based on knowledge (of language and facts).*

For the purposes of teaching professional translation it is important to distinguish the skill required from the linguistic and factual knowledge involved. As we saw, this skill encompasses four levels of language manipulation: conventions of form, interpretive analysis, interpretation of style, and textual organicity. I have used these four levels as a framework for the introductory translation course. The originality of a translator's work resides in his ability to conduct a rigorous analysis of a text and to write with grace and precision. These two abilities must form the cornerstones of a method for teaching this art of re-expression. It has been said that "Of the translator is demanded intelligence and eloquence in equal parts."[1]

The evolution of theoretical thought is often influenced by its applications. This is true of translation, in which "Each expansion of the translator's sphere of activity inevitably brings about a change in our very understanding of the translating operation, in its goal, and in the standards by which accuracy and fidelity to the original are judged."[2] We know from the

---

1. "Au traducteur s'impose une double tâche, également nécessaire, d'intelligence et d'éloquence." Zuber, *Les "Belles infidèles,"* p. 44.
2. "Chaque élargissement du champ d'activité des traducteurs mène inévitablement à une modification de la compréhension même de l'opération traduisante, de son but et des critères de l'exactitude, de la fidélité." Ljudskanov, *Traduction humaine*, vol. 1, p. 19. Historical types of translation are described on pp. 18-27.

history of translation that such a change took place as translators shifted their attention from the translation of religious texts, which tended to impose word-for-word translation, to the translation of secular texts, which set the tone for the translation of meaning. These two types of translation were succeeded by "free translation," which became widespread, particularly in literature and poetry, during the seventeenth and eighteenth centuries—the era of the "Belles infidèles." In the nineteenth century a new type of translation emerged, which could be termed "adequate translation," and which is still practised by most translators today. This type of translation seeks to preserve unity of form and content, remaining faithful not only to the words, the meaning, or some abstract ideal of beauty, as the three former types did, but to all aspects of the original text.

Today, two new factors play a predominant part in shaping our understanding of translation as a psycholinguistic activity: automation and the teaching of translation in professional schools. Machine translation projects have cast translation in a new light. Studies of the automation of semantic transfer from one language to another—a considerably less mechanistic operation than was naïvely supposed at first—have uncovered previously unsuspected problems and pushed the examination of the purely linguistic aspects of translation to ever greater depths. It is through this research that translation theory has been able to draw on advances in structural linguistics, information theory, and cybernetics.

Translation teaching, like machine translation, dates back no more than forty years. What were once schools of thought bringing together translators who shared a common conception of their craft have now given way to full-fledged educational institutions dispensing professional training. Both the automation and the teaching of translation stem from the urgent need to handle a workload whose growth has been exponential. An analysis of the thought processes involved in translation and of the workings of language in the context of semantic transfer is essential if the skill is to be taught. There had not previously been any need for such close examination of the cognitive process of translation. As noted in chapter 2, the appearance of the first theories of translation coincided with the establishment of the first professional schools.

Research into translation pedagogy can be as rich and original a source of insight as machine translation projects are. Teaching and research cannot be split at the university level, even in professional schools; they are not mutually exclusive but complementary. It is my hope that continued study on the pedagogy of translation will dispel the confusion still surrounding the theoretical investigation of this intellectual activity. Establishing a theoretical framework for the teaching of translation is a rigorous exercise that will lead to a reformulation of principles that have so far been taken for granted or at least to a narrowing of their scope. In other words, we will have to realize that principles valid for the translation of Biblical texts do not necessarily apply to all other types of texts. Theorists have already recognized the limitations of an exclusively linguistic approach to translation. They are departing from, or rather venturing beyond, the comparative model. The technique of contrasting two linguistic systems has produced many valid observations which can now be integrated into a true theory of translation based on discourse analysis. Such a theory would approach the text as an instance of language use within a given set of parameters.

A theory of translation that is not grounded in fact is unproductive, at least from a pedagogical point of view, while a collection of facts that are not incorporated into a coherent system can explain nothing, since facts have a solely illustrative value. Although it would no doubt be unrealistic to hope that a theory or method of translation could capture every aspect of the mental act of translating, there is no reason not to aim for this ideal. Teachers wishing to show their students how to transfer meaning from one language to another need a functional theory of translation. Such a theory would be grounded in practice, thus bringing together theorists and professional translators. Research in translation pedagogy can help to link the academic and professional worlds and serve as a catalyst for theoretical research. The teacher occupies an excellent observation post. The difficulties experienced by his students, and the discussions to which they give rise, can lend new impetus to translation theory. An interpretive theory of meaning can, for its part, pull pedagogy out of the rut of empiricism. Further studies in the pedagogy of translation will be so many building blocks in the construction of an interpretive and functional theory of translation.

Rebuilding the Breast

(Complete Text)

After the removal of her left breast because of cancer in 1970, Mrs. Joan Dawson, 54, of New York City, spent the next three years battling depression and a sense of loss. Then she decided to do something about it. Most women in the same situation turn to a psychiatrist. Mrs. Dawson (not her real name) went to her doctor and asked him to rebuild her missing breast. "I didn't want to be made into a sensational beauty," she explained. "I just wanted to be restored." Her surgeon was able to do just that. In two separate operations, he implanted a silicone-filled sac under the skin where the breast had been removed, then reduced the size of the other breast to make it more nearly resemble the new one. The result is not a duplication of Mrs. Dawson's pre-1970 figure, but she is delighted nevertheless. Says she: "I can finally look at myself in the mirror without wincing."

Since 1969 several hundred American women have undergone plastic surgery similar to Mrs. Dawson's—with increasingly satisfactory results. At a recent meeting at Rutgers Medical School, plastic surgeons predicted that the number of breast reconstructions would continue to rise. Self-examination and mass screening programs are detecting an increasing number of early breast cancers* before they spread; that makes it possible to perform less disfiguring operations than the standard radical mastectomy, in which not only the breast but the lymph nodes under the armpit and the muscles of the chest are removed. As a result, doctors predict that many of the 89,000 women who will undergo breast surgery this year will be able to take advantage of reconstructive surgery.

*When detected and treated by surgery in its earliest stage, breast cancer is nearly 100% curable, according to the American Cancer Society.

SURGICAL REVOLUTION

Doctors have been experimenting since the 1950s with techniques to rebuild amputated breasts with grafts of fatty tissues and implants. Their initial efforts were often unsuccessful. The earlier implants, which consisted of chemically inert plastics, were of a firmer consistency than normal breast tissue and were aesthetic failures; the reconstructed breast was often no more than a hard mound that was usually noticeably smaller than the remaining breast. The plastic, in fact, often shrank and became lumpy after implantation.

But since 1969 there has been a dramatic improvement in the quality of breast reconstruction. One reason was the development by Dr. Thomas Cronin of Houston of an improved implant. Another is the introduction of a newer though relatively little-used implant that overcomes most of the problems of earlier prostheses. It is divided into three compartments that reduce its tendency to shrink or collapse; the implant also has a fuzzy polyurethane covering that helps hold it in place against the chest wall. "It makes a dramatic difference," says Dr. Randolph Guthrie of New York's Memorial Hospital for Cancer and Allied Diseases.

So does another development, the perfection by Dr. Jon Olaf Strombeck of Stockholm of reduction mammoplasty, a technique for reducing the size of the breast. This can be used in reconstructive surgery to restore a measure of symmetry of the bust.

A third has been the growing acceptance of reconstruction by surgeons themselves. In the past, many doctors dismissed such surgery as frivolous (some major insurance companies still refuse to pay for such "vanity" operations). But now an increasing number of surgeons perform the initial amputation with reconstruction in mind, leaving as much skin as possible. When they can, they often attempt to save the nipple. Some doctors, however, oppose the idea, fearing the nipple may harbor cancer cells. Most agree, however, on the importance of at least making women who are facing surgery for breast cancer aware that reconstruction may be possible. "We don't spend enough time with them," says Dr. Henry Leis, chief of the breast service at New York Medical College. "We have to tell them the truth and give them hope for afterward."

GOOD RESULTS

When plans have been made in advance, reconstruction can be relatively simple. According to Dr. Reuben Snyderman of Princeton and Dr. Robert Goldwyn of Boston, a woman who has had a simple mastectomy (removal of the breast, but no other tissue) can usually be given a new breast in a single surgical session; all a doctor need do is slip in an implant. Women who have had more radical surgery require more complex procedures and must undergo several operations. Creation of a nipple by "sharing" the one from the intact breast, or the preferred method of building a new aureola (the rosette of tissue surrounding the nipple) out of skin removed from the labia, requires an additional operation or two.

Although reconstructive surgery seems safe, not even its most enthusiastic advocates recommend it for all breast-cancer patients. Only an estimated 20% of all women find it difficult to adjust to the deformity produced by mastectomy; a few even regard their scars as a "badge of courage." Doctors will not attempt reconstruction on women who have undergone excessive doses of radiotherapy after their initial operations: the X rays may scar too much tissue to permit successful reconstruction. They also wait at least six months after a mastectomy before attempting reconstruction: it takes that long for complete healing. But plastic surgeons see no reason to wait longer; cancer specialists say reconstruction need not interfere with the diagnosis of a recurrence—or its treatment.

Time, April 14, 1975.

APPENDIX 2

The Icy Grip Tightens

(First four paragraphs)

Never before in this century had the nation been so much at the mercy of its weather. Man, animal and machine in many parts of the country were immobilized under a heavy blanket of snow and ice. A dire shortage of natural gas—long predicted and long ignored—forced the closing of hundreds of schools and businesses and drove tens of thousands of people out of their unheated homes.

Economists estimate that millions have been laid off—in some cases only briefly—because of plant shutdowns. Just on the verge of recovering from its sustained pause, the economy has also been buffeted. The growth rate for the first quarter of 1977 has been scaled down half a percentage point, to 5%, because of the bad weather. President Carter's economic package of $31.2 billion, to be spread out over 20 months, has been jeopardized: a large chunk of the tax rebates will be eaten up by an extra $7 billion to $8 billion in fuel bills. On top of this, food costs are soaring as the cold blights Florida fruits and vegetables and farmers have to buy additional live-stock feed. Some economists figure that the inflation rate for the first quarter could reach 9%, compared with 4.2% in the final quarter of 1976.

If there is too much winter in some sections of the country, there is, strangely enough, too little elsewhere. With far less snowfall than usual, the West is suffering from a prolonged drought. A shortage of water is imperiling winter wheat and other crops; fears are growing that hydroelectric power will decrease in the spring. Water is already being rationed in parts of California (see following story). In Oregon, forest fires have broken out. "Some say the world will end in fire," wrote Robert Frost, "some say in ice." Last week Americans had their choice of disasters. If that is not enough, they soon may undergo trial by water. When the massive snow-drifts melt in the warming weather, torrential floods are expected to sweep many parts of the country.

As a Southerner, Jimmy Carter has experienced mostly mild winters. Moving north to the White House, he has been confronted, ironically enough, with fierce cold as his first crisis. He has responded with the activism he pledged. ''If there hadn't been an energy crisis,'' says an aide, ''we probably would have had to create one.'' That seems a high price to pay for a demonstration of presidential leadership, but there was no disputing the fact that Carter was moving fast and forcefully. He dramatized the crisis—and the presidential role in it—by hastily convening a Cabinet meeting, then taking a quick trip to frozen Pittsburgh. He declared eleven states disaster areas because of snow or drought, thus making them eligible for some form of federal assistance.

Time, February 14, 1977.

Pedagogical Objectives of the Introductory Course in Translation of Pragmatic Texts from English to French

1. Transcoded equivalents and translated equivalents
2. Sentence equivalents and contextual equivalents
3. Text explication
4. Annotated translation
5. Extracting key concepts
6. Interpretive analysis
7. Translation, retrieval of standard equivalents, and re-creation in context
8. Re-creation in context and reasoning by analogy
9. Reading between the lines—implied meanings
10. Breaking away from the structures of the original text
11. French superlative and English comparative
12. Use of noun constructions in French
13. Concision: defining instead of describing
14. Spatial constraints: translation of catalogues, photo captions, and side-by-side bilingual documents
15. Avoiding repetition
16. Metaphors
17. Deixis in English: "this"
18. Textual organicity
19. Paraphrasing
20. Avoiding translatorese
21. Clichés and expressions
22. Allusions
23. Revising for idiomaticity

Bibliography

For an updated and more exhaustive bibliography, see the *Bibliographie du traducteur/ Translator's Bibliography* published by the University of Ottawa Press in the same collection (Translation Studies, No. 6, 1987). It lists over two thousand books and articles on the subjects of translation in French, English, and Spanish; interpretation; terminology; and writing-skills development.

Bally, Charles. *Linguistique générale et linguistique française*. Berne, Francke, 1944.

Belloc, Hilaire. "On Translation," *The Bookman*, No. 74, 1931, pp. 32-39; 179-185.

Bénard, Jean-Paul, and Paul Horguelin. *Pratique de la traduction. Version générale*. Montréal, Linguatech, 1977.

Béziers, Monique, and Maurits Van Overbeke. *Le bilinguisme. Essai de définition et guide bibliographique*. Université de Louvain, Librairie universitaire, 1968 (Cahiers de l'Institut des langues vivantes, 13).

Bovy, F. "Codage et décodage du traducteur," *Le Linguiste*, Vol. 10, No. 3, 1964, pp. 5-8.

_____ . "Conclusions d'ordre pédagogique et méthodologique de la journée pédagogique du 17 mars 1972 pour les Instituts Belges de la traduction." Thème : "Méthodologie de la traduction," Jan. 1973.

_____ . "Processus et méthodologie de la traduction," Rapport de la journée pédagogique pour les Instituts Belges de la traduction, March 17, 1972.

Brislin, Richard W., ed. *Translation: Applications and Research*. New York, Gardner Press, 1976.

Brooks, Nelson. "The Meaning of Bilingualism Today," *Foreign Language Annuals*, Vol. 2, No. 3, 1969, pp. 304-309.

Buisseret, Irène de. *Deux langues, six idiomes. Manuel pratique de traduction de l'anglais au français : préceptes, procédés, exemples, glossaires, index*. Ottawa, Carlton-Green, 1975.

Buyssens, Eric. "Le langage et la logique—Le langage et la pensée," in *Le Langage*, published under the direction of André Martinet, Encyclopédie de la Pléiade, Gallimard, 1968, pp. 76-90.

Cary, Edmond. *La traduction dans le monde moderne*. Geneva, Georg & Cie, 1956.

Casagrande, J. B. "The Ends of Translation," *International Journal of American Linguistics*, Vol. 20, No. 4, 1954, pp. 335-340.

Catford, John Cunnison. *A Linguistic Theory of Translation: An Essay in Applied Linguistics*. London, Oxford University Press, 1965.

Charaudeau, P. "Sens et signification," *Cahiers de lexicologie*, Vol. 21, No. 2, 1972, pp. 9-21.

Charbonneau-Dagenais, Aline. "Essai de définition du bilinguisme," *Bulletin de l'Association canadienne de linguistique appliquée*, Vol. 4, No. 1, 1979, pp. 31-38.

Citroen, I. J. "Targets in Translator Training," *Meta*, Vol. 11, No. 4, 1966, pp. 139-144.

——————— . "Training Technical Translators," *Babel*, Vol. 1, No. 2, 1955, pp. 61-64.

Coindreau, Maurice-Edgar. *Mémoires d'un traducteur*. Paris, Gallimard, 1974.

Congrès mondial de la Fédération internationale des traducteurs. *La traduction, une profession/Translating, a Profession*. Proceedings of the 8th World Congress of the International Federation of Translators, Montreal, 1977, ed. Paul A. Horguelin. Montreal, Canadian Translators and Interpreters Council, 1978.

Cormier, Monique C. *Traduction technique et pédagogie*. Diss., Université de la Sorbonne Nouvelle (Paris III), 1986.

Darbelnet, Jean. "Caractérologie linguistique," *L'Actualité terminologique*, Vol. 10, No. 4, 1977, pp. 1-4; No. 5, pp. 1-4.

——————— . "La traduction raisonnée," *Meta*, Vol. 14, No. 3, 1969, pp. 135-140.

——————— . "Linguistique différentielle et traduction," *Meta*, Vol. 16, No. 1-2, 1971, pp. 17-24.

——————— . "Niveaux de la traduction," *Babel*, Vol. 23, No. 1, 1977, pp. 6-17.

——————— . "Pour une revalorisation des exercices de traduction dans l'étude des langues," *Culture*, Vol. 24, 1963, pp. 348-355.

——————— . "Réflexions sur la formation générale du traducteur," *Meta*, Vol. 11, No. 4, 1966, pp. 155-160.

——————— . "Traduction littérale ou traduction libre?", *Journal des Traducteurs*, Vol. 10, No. 4, 1965, pp. 154-157.

Dejean Le Féal, Karla. *Lectures et improvisations : Incidences de la forme de l'énonciation sur la traduction simultanée (français-allemand)*. Diss., Université de la Sorbonne Nouvelle (Paris III), 1978.

Delisle, Jean. *L'Analyse du discours comme méthode de traduction : Initiation à la traduction française de textes pragmatiques anglais, théorie et pratique*. Ottawa, University of Ottawa Press, 1980.

——————— . "Une discipline en quête d'une méthodologie," *L'Antenne* (Bulletin of the Société des traducteurs du Québec), Vol. 10, No. 6, 1979, pp. 2-3.

——————— . "Projet d'histoire de la traduction et de l'interprétation au Canada," *Meta*, Vol. 22, No. 1, 1977, pp. 66-71.

Dubois, Jean et al. *Dictionnaire de linguistique*. Paris, Larousse, 1973.

Dubuc, Robert. "L'apprentissage de la traduction à l'ère des méthodes actives," *Translatio*, Vol. 6, No. 3, 1967, pp. 65-67.

——————— . *Manuel pratique de terminologie*. Montréal, Linguatech, 1978.

Durieux, Christine. *Décomposition de la démarche propre à la traduction technique en vue de dégager les principes pour une pédagogie de la traduction*. Diss., Université de la Sorbonne Nouvelle (Paris III), 1984.

Duron, Jacques. *Langue française, Langue humaine*. Paris, Larousse, 1963.

Ebel, J. G. "Translation and Linguistics: A Search for Definitions," *The Incorporated Linguist*, Vol. 7, No. 3, 1968, pp. 50-54.

Etkind, Efim. "La stylistique comparée, base de l'art de traduire," *Babel*, Vol. 8, No. 1, 1967, pp. 23-30.

Evans, Richard I. *Jean Piaget: The Man and His Ideas*. Trans. Eleanor Duckworth. New York, E.P. Dutton and Co., 1973.

Exégèse et Traduction. Issue of *Études de linguistique appliquée*, No. 12. Paris, Didier, 1973.

Findlay, Ian F. *Translating*. London, Teach Yourself Books, 1971.

Flesch, Rudolf. "The Pursuit of Translation," in *The Art of Clear Thinking*. London, Collier-Macmillan, 1972 (copyright 1951), pp. 63-71.

Fowler, H. W. *A Dictionary of Modern English Usage*. London, Oxford University Press, 1926.

Fuller, Frederick *The Translator's Handbook*. London, Colin Smythe; University Park, Penn., Pennsylvania State University Press, 1904.

Gachechiladze, G. R. "Training Translators at the University," *Babel*, Vol. 11, No. 4, 1965, pp. 154-155.

Galisson, R. and D. Coste. *Dictionnaire de didactique des langues*. Paris, Librairie Hachette, 1976.

Garcia-Landa, Mariano. *Les déviations délibérées de la littéralité en interprétation de conférence*. Diss., Université de la Sorbonne Nouvelle (Paris III), 1978.

Gasse, Yvon. "Contextual Transposition in Translating Research Instruments," *Meta*, Vol. 18, No. 3, pp. 295-307.

Gerver, David, and H. W. Sinaiko, eds. *Language, Interpretation and Communication*. Proceedings of the NATO Symposium held at the Giorgio Cini Foundation, Venice, Sept. 26–Oct. 1, 1977. New York, Plenum Press, 1978.

Ghenet-Hottois, Michèle. "Contribution à une méthodologie de la composition," in *Dix années de linguistique théorique et appliquée*. Ministère de l'Éducation Nationale, Université de l'État de Mons. Mons, 1973, pp. 103-121.

Gouadec, Daniel. *Comprendre et traduire. Techniques de la version*. Paris, Bordas, 1974.

Grandjouan, Jacques Olivier. *Les Linguicides*. Paris, Didier, 1971.

Harris, Brian. "La traductologie, la traduction naturelle, la traduction automatique et la sémantique," *Cahiers de linguistique*, No. 2, Université du Québec à Montréal, 1973, pp. 133-146.

—————. "The Importance of Natural Translation," Revised text of a paper read to the AILA World Congress, Stuttgart, August 1975.

—————. "Toward a Science of Translation," *Meta*, Vol. 22, No. 1, 1977, pp. 90-92.

—————, and Bianca Sherwood. "Translating as an Innate Skill," Paper read at the NATO Symposium on Language, Interpretation and Communication, Venice, September 26-30, 1977.

Hartmann, R. R. and F. C. Stork. "The Place of Grammar and Translation in the Teaching of Modern Languages," *The Incorporated Linguist*, Vol. 3, No. 3, 1964, pp. 73-75.

Hendrickx, Paul V. "Language Teaching and Teaching Translation," *Babel*, Vol. 18, No. 13, 1972, pp. 14-20.

—————. "Should We Teach Translation?" *Babel*, Vol. 21, No. 3, 1975, pp. 101-106.

Holmes, James S. "Translation Theory, Translation Studies, and the Translator," in *La traduction, une profession/Translating, a Profession*. Proceedings of the 8th World Congress of the International Federation of Translators, 1977, ed. Paul A. Horguelin. Montreal, The Canadian Translators and Interpreters Council, 1978, pp. 55-61.

Horguelin, Paul A. *Pratique de la révision*. Montréal, Linguatech, 1978.

House, Juliane, "A Model for Assessing Translation Quality," *Meta*, Vol. 12, No. 2, 1977, pp. 103-109.

Howder, Murray et al. "Academic Training of Translators: A Debatable Issue," *Federal Linguist*, Vol. 5, No. 1-2, 1973, pp. 2-17.

Jacobson, Roman. "On Linguistic Aspects of Translation," in *On Translation*, ed. Reuben Arthur Brower. Cambridge, Harvard University Press, 1959, pp. 232-239.

Jumpelt, R. M. "Methodological Approaches to Science Translation," in *La qualité en matière de traduction/Quality in Translation*. Proceedings of the 3rd Congress of the International Federation of Translators (FIT), 1963, ed. E. Cary and R.M. Jumpelt. New York, Macmillan, 1963, pp. 267-281.

_____ . "Quality in Scientific and Technical Translation," *Babel*, Vol. 5, No. 2, 1959, pp. 107-109.

Kelly, Louis G. *The True Interpreter. A History of Translation Theory and Practice in the West*. Oxford, Basil Blackwell, 1979.

Kirstein, Bone H.-J. "Reducing Negative Transfer: Two Suggestions for the Use of Translation," *Modern Language Journal*, Vol. 6, No. 2, pp. 75-78.

Labov, William. *Sociolinguistic Patterns*. Philadelphia, University of Pennsylvania Press, 1972.

Ladmiral, Jean-René. "La traduction dans l'institution pédagogique," *Langage*, No. 28, 1972, pp. 8-39.

_____ . *"Traduire : théorèmes pour la traduction*, Petite bibliothèque Payot, No. 366. Paris, Payot, 1979.

Landsberg, Marge E. "Translation Theory: An Appraisal of Some General Problems," *Meta*, Vol. 21, No. 4, 1976, pp. 235-251.

Larose, Robert. *Théories contemporaines de la traduction*. Québec, Les Presses de l'Université du Québec, 1987.

Lederer, Marianne. *La traduction simultanée, fondements théoriques*. Université de Lille III, Service de reproduction des thèses, 1980.

_____ . "La traduction : transcoder ou réexprimer?", *Études de linguistique appliquée*, No. 12, 1973, pp. 7-25.

_____ . "Synecdoque et traduction," *Études de linguistique appliquée*, No. 24, 1976, pp. 13-41.

Levy, Jiri. "Will Translation Theory be of Use to Translators?", in *Ubersetzen*. Athenaum Verlag, Frankfurt, 1965, pp. 77-82.

Ljudskanov, Alexander. "À propos des *Problèmes théoriques de la traduction*," *T. A. Informations*, No. 1, 1968, pp. 107-112.

_____ . "A Semiotic Approach to the Theory of Translation," trans. Brian Harris, *Language Sciences*, No. 35, 1975, pp. 5-9.

_____ . *Traduction humaine et traduction mécanique*, 2 vols, Documents de linguistique quantitative 2,4. Paris, Dunod, 1969.

Lonergan, Bernard. "Merging Horizons: System, Common Sense, Scholarship," *Cultural Hermeneutics*, Vol. 1, 1973, pp. 87-99.

Long, Donald F. "Quality in Translation," *Journal des traducteurs*, Vol. 5, No. 1, 1960, pp. 7-9.

Maingueneau, Dominique. *Initiation aux méthodes de l'analyse du discours. Problèmes et perspectives*. Paris, Librairie Hachette, 1976.

Malinowski, Bronislav. "Théorie ethnographique du langage," in *Les Jardins de corail*, trans. and intro. Pierre Clinquart. Paris, F. Maspero, 1974, pp. 237-314.

Marouzeau, Jules. *Lexique de la terminologie linguistique français, allemand, anglais*. 2nd ed., Paris, Geuthner, 1944.

Martinet, André. *Éléments de linguistique générale*, Coll. V2, Paris, Armand Colin, 1967.

_____ ed. *Le Langage*, Coll. de la Pléiade. Paris, Gallimard, 1968.

Matthews-Bresky, R.J.H. "Translation as a Testing Device," *English Language Teaching*, Vol. 28, No. 1, 1972, pp. 58-65.

Melchuk, Igor. "Théorie de langage, théorie de traduction," *Meta*, Vol. 23, No. 4, 1978, pp. 271-302.

Milligan, E. E. "Some Principles and Techniques of Translation," *The Modern Language Journal*, Vol. 41, No. 2, 1967, pp. 66-71.

Moirand, Sophie. "Approche globale des textes écrits," *Études de linguistique appliquée*, No. 23, 1976, pp. 87-104.

Mounin, Georges. "La notion de qualité en matière de traduction littéraire," in *La qualité en matière de traduction/Quality in Translation*. Proceedings of the 3rd Congress of the International Federation of Translators (FIT), 1963, ed. E. Cary and R. M. Jumpelt. New York, Macmillan, 1963, pp. 50-57.

_____ . *Les belles infidèles*. Paris, Cahiers du Sud, 1955.

_____ . *Les problèmes théoriques de la traduction*. Paris, Gallimard, 1963.

_____ . *Linguistique et traduction*. Brussels, Dessart & Mardaga, 1976.

Newmark, Peter. "An Approach to Translation," *Babel*, Vol. 19, No. 1, 1973, pp. 3-19.

_____ . "Communicative and Semantic Translation," *Babel*, Vol. 23, No. 4, 1977, pp. 163-180.

_____ . "Further Propositions on Translation," *The Incorporated Linguist*, Vol. 13, No. 2 and 3, 1974. Part 1, pp. 34-42; Part 2, pp. 62-72.

_____ . "Some Notes on Translation and Translators," *The Incorporated Linguist*, Vol. 8, No. 4, 1969, pp. 79-85.

_____ . "The Theory and the Craft of Translation," *Language Teaching and Linguistics: Abstracts*, Vol. 19, No. 1. Cambridge University Press, 1976, pp. 5-16.

_____ . "Twenty-Three Restricted Rules of Translation," *The Incorporated Linguist*, Vol. 12, No. 1, 1973, pp. 9-15.

Nida, Eugene A. "A Framework for the Analysis and Evaluation of Theories of Translation," in *Translation: Applications and Research*, ed. R. W. Brislin. New York, Gardner Press, 1976, pp. 47-91.

_____ . *Language Structure and Translation Essays*, comp. and intro. A. S. Dil. Stanford, Cal., Stanford University Press, 1975.

_____ . "Meaning and Translation," *The Bible Translator*, Vol. 8, No. 3, 1957, pp. 97-108.

_____ . "The Nature of Dynamic Equivalence in Translating," *Babel*, Vol. 23, No. 3, 1977, pp. 99-103.

_____ . *Toward a Science of Translating, with Special Reference to Principles and Procedures Involved in Bible Translating*. Leiden, E. J. Brill, 1964.

_____ . "Translation," in *Current Trends in Linguistics*, ed. T. Sebeok, Vol. 12. The Hague, Mouton, 1974, pp. 1045-1068.

_____ and Charles Taber. *The Theory and Practice of Translation*. Leiden, E. J. Brill, 1969.

Pergnier, Maurice. "L'envers des mots," *Études de linguistique appliquée*, No. 24, 1976, pp. 92-126.

_____ . *Les fondements sociolinguistiques de la traduction*. Atelier reproduction des thèses, Université de Lille III, 1978.

_____ . "Traduction et théorie linguistique," *Études de linguistique appliquée*, No. 12, 1973, pp. 26-38.

Perret, Jacques. "Traduction et parole," in *Problèmes de la traduction littéraire*. Papers read at a seminar during the academic year 1973-74. Louvain, Bibliothèque de l'Université, 1975, pp. 9-27.

Piaget, Jean. *The Psychology of Intelligence*. Trans. Malcolm Piercy and D.E. Berlyne. London, Routledge and Kegan Paul, 1950.

Poisson, Jacques. "La traduction, facteur d'acculturation," in *La traduction, une profession/Translating, a Profession*. Proceedings of the 8th World Congress of the International Federation of Translators, Montreal, 1977, ed. Paul A. Horguelin. Montreal, The Canadian Translators and Interpreters Council, 1978, pp. 281-291.

Robert, Paul. *Dictionnaire alphabétique et analogique de la langue française*. Paris, Société du Nouveau Littré, 1974.

Robert-Collins Dictionnaire français-anglais, anglais-français. 2nd ed. Paris, Dictionnaires Le Robert. London, Collins, 1987.

Saussure, Ferdinand de. *Course in General Linguistics*. Trans. and intro. Wade Baskin. New York, McGraw-Hill, 1966.

Savory, Theodore Horace. *The Art of Translation*. London, J. Cafe, 1968.

Seleskovitch, Danica. "Interpretation, A Psychological Approach to Translating," in *Translation: Applications and Research*, ed. R. W. Brislin. New York, Gardner Press, 1976, pp. 92-116.

_____ . *Interpreting for International Conferences*. Washington, Pen & Booth, 1978. Originally published as *L'interprète dans les conférences internationales* (Paris, Minard, Lettres Modernes, 1968).

_____ . *Langage, langues et mémoire*. Paris, Minard, Lettres Modernes, 1975.

_____ . "Language and Cognition," in *Language, Interpretation and Communication*, ed. D. Gerver and H.W. Sinaiko. New York, Plenum Press, 1978, pp. 333-341.

_____ . *L'interprète dans les conférences internationales*. Paris, Minard, Lettres Modernes, 1975.

_____ . "Traduire : de l'expérience aux concepts," *Études de linguistique appliquée*, No. 24, 1976, pp. 64-91.

_____ . "Vision du monde et traduction," *Études de linguistique appliquée*, No. 12, 1973, pp. 105-109.

_____ . "Why Interpreting Is Not Tantamount to Translating Languages," *The Incorporated Linguist*, Vol. 16, No. 2, 1977, pp. 27-33.

_____ , and Marianne Lederer. *Interpréter pour traduire*. Publications de la Sorbonne, Paris, Didier Érudition, 1984.

Shillan, David. "An Application of Contrastive Linguistics," *Meta*, Vol. 15, No. 3, 1970, pp. 161-163.

_____ . "Contrastive Linguistics and the Translator," *The Incorporated Linguist*, Vol. 10, No. 1, 1971, pp. 10-13.

Simpson, Ekundayo. "Methodology in Translation Criticism," *Meta*, Vol. 20, No. 4, 1975, pp. 251-262.

Slama-Cazacu, Tatiana. *Langage et contexte*. The Hague, Mouton, 1961.

Smeaton, B. Hunter. "Translation as an Alternate Mode of Expression," *Translators' Journal*, Vol. 8, No. 2, 1963, pp. 39-45.

Sperber, Dan. "Rudiments de rhétorique cognitive," in *Poétique*. Paris, Le Seuil, 1975, pp. 389-415.

Spolsky, Bernard. "Comparative Stylistics and the Principle of Economy," *Translators' Journal*, Vol. 7, No. 3, 1962, pp. 79-83.

Steiner, George. *After Babel: Aspects of Language and Translation*. London, Oxford University Press, 1975.

Thiéry, Christopher. *Le bilinguisme chez les interprètes de conférence professionnels*. Diss., Université de la Sorbonne Nouvelle (Paris III), 1975.

Tournier, Michel. *Le vent Paraclet*. Paris, Gallimard, 1977.

La traduction. Issue of *Langages*, No. 28, 1972. Paris, Didier/Larousse.

Traduire : les idées et les mots. Issue of *Études de linguistique appliquée*, No. 24, Paris, Didier, 1976.

Uhlenbeck, E. M. "On the Distinction Between Linguistics and Pragmatics," in *Language, Interpretation and Communication*, ed. D. Gerver and H. W. Sinaiko. New York, Plenum Press, 1978, pp. 185-198.

Ullmann, Stephen. *Semantics: An Introduction to the Science of Meaning*. Oxford, Basil Blackwell, 1962. Reprinted 1972.

UNESCO. "Draft Recommendation on the Legal Protection of Translators and Translations and on the Practical Means of Improving the Conditions of Translators," General Conference, 19th Session, Document 19C/30, Appendix 1, Nairobi, 1976.

Ure, Jean. "Types of Translation and Translatability," *Babel*, Vol. 10, No. 1, 1964, pp. 5-11.

Vázquez-Ayora, Gerardo. *Introducción a la traductología*. Washington, D.C., Georgetown University Press, 1977.

Vinay, Jean-Paul. *Cahier d'exercices/Work Book* for *Stylistique comparée du français et de l'anglais*. Montréal, Beauchemin, No. 1, 1968; No. 2, 1972.

_____ . "La langue neutre et la technique du 'démontage' en traduction," *Stylistique et linguistique*, Vol. 2, No. 4. Montréal, Département de linguistique, L'Université de Montréal, 1956, pp. 46-58.

_____ . "La traduction littéraire est-elle un genre à part?" *Meta*, Vol. 14, No. 1, 1969, pp. 5-21.

_____ . "Les déictiques," *Journal des traducteurs*, Vol. 1, No. 4, 1956, pp. 91-94.

_____ . "Peut-on enseigner la traduction?", *Journal des traducteurs*, Vol. 2, No. 4, 1957, pp. 141-148.

_____ . "Regards sur l'évolution des théories de la traduction depuis vingt ans," *Meta*, Vol. 20, No. 1, 1975, pp. 7-27.

_____ . "The Theory of Translation: Myth or Reality," in *Translation and Interpretation: The Multi-Cultural Context. A Symposium*, ed. Michael S. Batts. Vancouver, CAUTG, 1975, pp. 35-45.

_____ . "Vision comparative et vision absolue," *Journal des traducteurs*, Vol. 1, No. 3, 1956, pp. 59-63.

_____ , and Jean Darbelnet. *Stylistique comparée du français et de l'anglais. Méthode de traduction*. Paris, Didier, 1958.

Wandruszka, Mario. "Nos langues : structures instrumentales, structures mentales," *Meta*, Vol. 16, No. 1-2, 1971, pp. 7-16.

Weightman, J. G. "Translation as a Linguistic Exercise," *English Language Teaching*, Vol. 5, 1950, pp. 69-76.

Weissman, Stanley N. *Foundations of a Theory of Translation For Natural Languages*. Diss., Columbia University, 1965. (Available through University Microfilms, Ann Arbor, Michigan, U.S.A.)

Wilss, Wolfram. "Curricular Planning," *Meta*, Vol. 22, No. 2, 1977, pp. 117-124.

Zuber, Roger. *Les "Belles infidèles" et la formation du goût classique*. Paris, Armand Colin, 1968.